D1000406

# Safe Encounters

*ALSO BY BEVERLY WHIPPLE*

*The G Spot and Other Recent Discoveries about Human Sexuality*
(coauthored with Alice Kahn Ladas and John D. Perry)

*ALSO BY GINA OGDEN*

*When a Family Needs Therapy*
(coauthored with Anne Zevin)

# SAFE ENCOUNTERS

## How Women Can Say Yes to Pleasure and No to Unsafe Sex

BEVERLY WHIPPLE, Ph.D., R.N.
and GINA OGDEN, Ph.D.

McGraw-Hill Book Company

New York St. Louis San Francisco
Hamburg Mexico Toronto

*Even though the authors believe the information in this book to be as complete, accurate, and up-to-date as possible, any application of the recommendations set forth in the following pages is at the reader's discretion and risk. This book is not intended to replace the services of a physician, who should be consulted regarding any medical questions you may have.*



1 2 3 4 5 6 7 8 9 FGR FGR 8 9 2 1 0 9 8

ISBN 0-07-069519-9

**Library of Congress Cataloging-in Publication Data**

Whipple, Beverly.
Safe encounters.

Bibliography: p.
1. Sex instruction for women—United States.
2. Safe sex in AIDS prevention—United States.
3. Women—United States—Sexual behavior. I. Ogden, Gina. II. Title.
HQ46.W48 1989 613.9'5'088042 88-869
ISBN 0-07-069519-9

Illustrations by Judith Lerner
Book design by Patrice Fodero

For
Jim, Allen, and Susan,
Philip and Cathy

BODY DUST
EDIBLE CONDOM
TASTY
LOW-CAL
EDIBLE UNDIES
VAGINAL CONTRACEPTIVE FOAM
NONOXYNOL-9
EROTICA
TROJANENZ
SLIPPE
3 CONDOMS
Judith '88

# Contents

*Acknowledgments* ix
*Introduction* xi
*A User's Guide to Terms and Concepts* xv

**Part One. Saying Yes to Pleasure and No to Unsafe Sex**

1. Safe Sex Begins with You: Revamping Your Attitudes 3
2. The Right Relationship Is a Safe Relationship 19
3. Safe Sex Turns Women On: Options Other than Intercourse 43
4. The Latex Factor: Doing It, Talking about It, and Liking It 64
5. What about Flying Solo? 96
6. Teaching Your Partner to Play 120

**Part Two. Facts at Your Fingertips**

7. Answers to Questions about AIDS and Other STDs 147
8. The Birds, the Bees, and the Condoms: Talking with Your Children about Sex and AIDS 176
9. Help—and How to Ask for It 193

*Notes and Suggested Readings* 208
*Bibliography* 212
*Index* 216

# *List of Illustrations*

Putting a condom on a flaccid penis 72
Putting a condom on an erect penis 72
Rolling a condom to the base of a penis 73
Pinching a condom during its removal to retain fluid in the tip 73
Using latex gloves and a dental dam 80
The external female genitalia 104

# Acknowledgments

AIDS is a heartrending subject to research. We wish to thank those who helped and encouraged us every inch of the way.

Jo Chaffee lived with all aspects of this project and gave the book not only word power, but also heart.

Jim Whipple kept us on-line with endless patience and good humor.

Jim Ramey initiated our collaboration by introducing us many years ago and by inciting us to see the possibilities in this project; Patricia Pearlman openly shared her expertise; Judith Lerner appeared when we needed just the right artist with just the right touch; Terry Jenkins taught us to tame the word processor; Dell Williams lent us half her store.

Our students, clients, colleagues, family and friends have kept us on track, and offered many of the insights that breathe life into this book. We offer special thanks to: Dr. Frank Addiego, Gaea Aeolus, Pat Bessey, Robin Birdfeather, Sharon Marr Brown, Dr. Carol Cobb-Nettleton, Tassi Crabb, Vickie DiFabio, Peg W. Eby, Elaine Lavalle Freeman, Vivian Heiler, Janice Irvine, Terry Jenkins, Tom Jenkins, Mimi Katzenbach, Ethel Kellogg, Dr. Barry Komisaruk, Honor Moore, Nancy Perman, Betty Ramey, Dr. James Ramey, Maura Ryan, Cathy Saunders, Barbara Scheupele, Becky Scotten, Dr. George Sellmer, Pepita Seth, Dr. William Stayton, June Sweeten, Mary Lee Tatum, Beryl Title, Beatrice Hoehne Walsh, Dr. Martin Weisberg, Allen Whipple, Jim Whipple, Susan Whipple, and Anne Zevin.

Our agent and editor have been friends as well as professionals: Heide Lange believed in us both, and brought us together on this project; Bobbi Mark recognized the need for a positive approach to a devastating problem, and consistently helped us to focus on clarity.

A friend and former student of Beverly's was a special inspiration: Shortly before he died of AIDS he asked if she could spread the word. Danny, we hope this helps others find sexual satisfaction—and avoid the suffering you experienced.

Finally, we wish to acknowledge each other. Working together has been a pleasure.

# Introduction

What do we do in an age that's demonstrating to us that if the bomb doesn't get us, the AIDS virus will?

Researchers predict that in a few years, many millions of people will be infected with the AIDS virus. Women are the fastest growing risk group in the United States and may ultimately make up half of all AIDS cases, as they now do in Haiti and central Africa. But despite a dawning awareness that the number of women with AIDS is growing, little media space is given to the nitty-gritty specifics of how women can keep themselves safe. Generalized advice about monogamy, celibacy, or condoms is not the whole answer.

The spread of AIDS dictates that women's lives will increasingly depend on learning new patterns of dating, courtship, cohabitation, and marriage. AIDS is deadly and has no known cure, but it is preventable; each of us can keep from contracting the AIDS virus by educating ourselves and changing our patterns of having sex. Women can no longer afford to engage in old sexual habits, especially the habit of unprotected intercourse.

AIDS crosses barriers of class, race, and culture and raises questions that wrack the minds of women in all sorts of situations:

"Just what is safe sex? Am I at risk? Should I be tested? How do I protect myself? What if I get pregnant?"

"If I'm not married, does that mean I should be celibate to be safe? How do I talk about safe sex with a partner? Can I still have fun and be spontaneous if I stop to take precautions? Exactly how do I use condoms? Suppose my partner doesn't want to use them? Is safety selfish?"

"How do I tell my daughter about keeping safe? What do I tell her about trusting men? How do I talk with my friends?"

*Safe Encounters* answers these questions and many others. It fully acknowledges the epidemic aspects of AIDS and aims to dispel irrational fears. It discusses explicitly how women can enjoy active, loving sex lives in safety and health. It goes beyond morality and mechanics to provide a guide to sensuous sex for women and their partners.

The book is divided into two parts. Part I, "Saying Yes to Pleasure and No to Unsafe Sex," offers responsible and pleasurable approaches to sexual interactions with yourself and your partner(s). Part II, "Facts at Your Fingertips," answers questions about AIDS and other sexually transmitted diseases and includes chapters on how to talk to children and where to find help when you need it.

Why is *Safe Encounters* addressed particularly to women rather than equally to women and men?

First of all, women experience sex differently from men and often have different sexual values. These differences need to be directly addressed to reach women and help them change to safer sexual patterns. For instance, issues of partnership may be as important to women's satisfaction as physical contact and orgasm. *Safe Encounters* spells out how women can choose safer partners and make love in safer ways. It teaches techniques to enable women to judge whether they're in a safe situation with a safe partner. It explores the emotional and relational aspects of safe sex, with how-to's and suggestions for self-care so that women can take charge of their own wellbeing.

In addition, we feel that women have special concerns about sexual responsibility and pleasure and that the threat of AIDS heightens these concerns.

Sexual responsibility is difficult for many women to practice because they're embarrassed to express themselves assertively about health and safety—this is especially true of women who expect men to be the initiators and experts. And sexual pleasure has been traditionally taboo for women. Consequently, many women today opt for unsafe sexual practices because they lack information about pleasures that might be perfectly safe. They also lack the permission to let go and enjoy these pleasures.

*Safe Encounters* demonstrates that pleasurable sex does not have to mean danger and that safe sex does not have to mean deprivation. In fact, it teaches readers that once they move beyond the myth that intercourse is the goal of all sexual encounters, or even that sex means genital contact, there are literally 1,001 ways to sexual satisfaction.

The new patterns of sexual behavior suggested in *Safe Encounters* offer women ways to assume responsibility for their own pleasure and safety. The book provides information that will allow women to think about sex creatively, choose partners differently, relate to their partners more meaningfully, educate their children more accurately, and find delightful ways to incorporate safe sex into their lives.

Although the information is addressed specifically to women, men will also find it helpful and enhancing to their relationships with women.

It is our belief that women want safe sex. Women who follow the guidelines offered here will not only be physically safer, they'll also feel better about themselves and have healthier relationships.

# A User's Guide to Terms and Concepts

## *A Note on "Safe" and "Safer"*

When we use the words "safe sex," we are referring to thoughts, fantasies, feelings, and physical activities that do not involve the exchange of body fluids. We are also referring to intercourse between partners who are not infected with the AIDS virus or with any other sexually transmitted diseases (STDs).

Specific guidelines for ensuring safe sex are offered in Chapters 1, 2, 3, 5, and 6.

When we use the words "safer sex," we are using the current phrase to describe sex where there are risk conditions that are being dealt with. Specifically, this means using condoms or other barriers during anal or vaginal sex with a partner you're not absolutely sure is free of the AIDS virus or any other STDs.

Specific guidelines for ensuring safer sex are offered in Chapter 4.

## *Safe-Sex Evaluation*

How do you know what's safe and what's risky? First of all, any sexual practice is free of the risk of AIDS if neither you nor your partner is infected.

Before you read this book, you can use the following checklist to give yourself a quick overview of how safe your behaviors are if there is any possibility that either you or your partner is HIV-positive.

| *Safe-Sex Behaviors* | *Safer-Sex Behaviors (Somewhat risky)* | *High-Risk Behaviors* |
|---|---|---|
| Holding hands<br>Hugging<br>Caressing<br>Body massage<br>Bathing together<br>Masturbation<br>Mutual masturbation<br>Using personal sex toys<br>Sensuous feeding<br>Fantasizing<br>Sharing fantasies<br>Watching erotic movies<br>Reading erotic books and magazines<br>Telephone sex | French kissing<br>Vaginal intercourse, using latex condom and spermicide with nonoxynol-9<br>Anal intercourse, using latex condom<br>Fellatio (oral sex on a man), using latex condom<br>Cunnilingus (oral sex on a woman), using dental dam<br>Manual stimulation of vagina or anus, using latex gloves | Vaginal intercourse without using latex condom and spermicide with nonoxynol-9<br>Anal intercourse without using latex condom<br>Fellatio without using latex condom<br>Cunnilingus without using dental dam<br>Manual stimulation of anus or vagina without using latex gloves<br>Exchanging blood<br>Sharing sex toys without proper cleaning<br>Sucking breasts of lactating woman |

# *Glossary of Commonly Used Terms and Abbreviations*

**Abstinence** No sexual contact with another person.

**AIDS (Acquired Immunodeficiency Syndrome)** A viral infection that destroys part of the body's immune system, leaving the body unable to fight disease.

**Antibodies** Proteins produced in the blood in response to a foreign organism. Antibodies to the AIDS virus indicate that infection by the AIDS virus has occurred.

**ARC (AIDS-Related Complex)** A disease condition caused by infection with the AIDS virus, but with none of the specific life-threatening illnesses used to diagnose AIDS. It usually precedes AIDS.

**Body Fluids** Fluids manufactured by the body. Although the AIDS virus has been found in most body fluids, those that are thought to be most likely to transmit the virus to another person are semen and blood. Other body fluids which may transmit AIDS, but which are less likely to, are vaginal secretions, saliva, and breast milk.

**Celibacy** No genital contact with another person.

**ELISA Test** A blood test that indicates the presence of antibodies to the AIDS virus. It does not detect the disease AIDS but only indicates whether viral infection has occurred.

**High-Risk Behaviors** Activities that increase the risk of transmitting the AIDS virus. These activities include anal or vaginal intercourse without a condom, oral-anal contact, semen in the mouth, manual-anal penetration, sharing intravenous needles, contact with blood, sharing sex toys that have come in contact with semen or blood.

**HIV (Human Immunodeficiency Virus)** The usual name for the virus that causes AIDS.

**IV Drugs** Drugs like heroin or cocaine that are injected into the bloodstream intravenously, with a hypodermic needle.

**Monogamy** Sex with one partner exclusively.

**Opportunistic Infections** Infections that cannot be fought off by weakened immune systems.

**Safe Sex** Sexual activities that do not involve the exchange of body fluids.

**Safer Sex** Sexual activities that exchange body fluids but use a latex barrier and possibly a spermicide to inhibit that exchange.

**Spermicide** A substance that kills sperm and is used as a contraceptive. One spermicide, nonoxynol-9, has been shown to kill the AIDS virus in test tubes.

**STD (Sexually Transmitted Disease)** An infectious disease that is passed from one person to another through intimate sexual contact. Some STDs may be transmitted from an infected pregnant mother to her fetus.

**Western Blot** A blood test used to confirm the results of a positive ELISA test. This is a more accurate and more expensive antibody test than the ELISA.

# Part One

## Saying Yes to Pleasure and No to Unsafe Sex

# CHAPTER 1

## *Safe Sex Begins with You: Revamping Your Attitudes*

Betty is 28 and single. She lives in a small town, and when she asked her doctor what she should do to protect herself from getting AIDS, he assured her:

"Listen, if you meet a nice guy and he's not from the city and he says he doesn't have AIDS, you don't have to worry about a thing."

"That was six months ago," sighs Betty, "and I know a little more about the situation now. But I'm feeling confused and angry and very scared.

"I haven't been promiscuous or anything, but I've slept with a few different guys over the last years without protecting myself. And sure, they were nice guys from the country, but the awful thing is you don't really know who has it or where it begins. Maybe those guys have slept with other people who had it. Nobody knows where it comes from. It seems like some kind of germ warfare."

Betty made herself literally sick with worry that she might have contracted the AIDS virus. She begged a second doctor for a diagnostic blood test. He scoffed at the idea that she might have AIDS and advised her not to get tested. He confided to her that other patients of his had been dropped by their insurance companies when their tests had been discovered and that one had even lost his job.

By calling the department of health in the city, Betty located a center that performed confidential testing. She was informed that to test with accuracy, she would first have to remain celibate for six months. Because of a tremendous backlog, the test would then take an additional three weeks to process.

"And so I'm sitting out my celibacy period and going nuts. And it's not just when I'm awake. My old invasion nightmares came back—the ones that started when my mother died of cancer. Last night I dreamt heavy machines were bulldozing down my house and the construction crew crashed through my bedroom window wearing pink bowling shirts.

"How do I deal with the anxiety of the situation? Even if I test negative, how do I find out what's really safe? And when I decide I want to start going out again, how do I bring the subject up? And if I do, how do I know he'd tell me the truth?

"Honestly, I'm so confused about the whole thing, I don't know what to do. Sometimes I think it would be easier just to stay home and watch the late show on Saturday night. But I get so lonely."

Betty echoes concerns felt by millions of women without permanent and trusted monogamous sexual partners in this age of AIDS and other sexually transmitted diseases.

Where do women get information about what to do?

AIDS has shocked world consciousness enough so that the media are full of articles and stories. There are books and pamphlets, public-interest advertising, and discussions in schools and universities. But while these communications stress the *safe* or *safer* part of safe sex, they almost all omit the part that has to do with sex.

They advise celibacy or abstinence without discussing that most people actively seek out some kind of sexual expression all of their lives, from birth until death.

They advise monogamy without acknowledging researchers' estimates that more than half of all monogamous partnerships may experience outside sexual affairs and that most of the women who get AIDS through sexual contact get it through repeated monogamous intercourse with an infected partner.

They advise condoms, but then they stop without showing exactly how to use them, or demonstrating how to communicate about them, or teaching how to carry out the sexual part of your relationship in pleasurable and safer ways.

And no education system that we're aware of tells women the how-to's of developing a pleasurable and safer attitude about sexuality.

This book is addressed to women who are concerned about AIDS and also to women who have trouble believing that the AIDS epidemic can affect them: single women, women contemplating pregnancy, young women newly on the dating scene, mothers needing to inform their children, women whose partners have died, and all the women in monogamous relationships whose partners have had affairs. And it's addressed to women's partners—both those who are concerned and those who deny that AIDS can affect them.

We begin with the premise that there is no such thing as totally safe sex with an infected partner. And we affirm that sexual pleasure is still attainable—with responsibility.

We offer practical suggestions that we hope will make coping with the fact of AIDS not such an overwhelming task that you give up before you begin. In fact, we'd like to issue a note of optimism to Betty and all the other women whose sex lives are somehow touched by AIDS. You can make all your sexual encounters not only safer but more pleasurable by reframing your attitudes about sex and by developing a new sexual etiquette. This new etiquette is based on a very old concept: loving yourself enough to take the measures necessary to keep yourself from harm.

## *A New Etiquette of Sex*

If your old mode was to jump right into bed and have intercourse, that won't work anymore. Or if you're new to sex, or if you're newly dating after an extended monogamous relationship, you may be at a loss as to how to proceed safely.

The days are gone when women can actively or passively participate in slam-bam-thank-you-ma'am encounters. The AIDS epidemic has made it a matter of life and death that we change the old sexual expectation and habit of unprotected intercourse. To keep ourselves safe, we must develop new habits with each of our partners except those who can prove beyond a shadow of a doubt that they are HIV-negative.

In practical terms, this means we must be scrupulously careful to practice safer sex in all relationships except those that are long-term and monogamous—and absolutely trustworthy.

It's essential to stress here the importance of trustworthy monogamy, even among loving, lifelong partnerships. When monogamous partners have affairs, most of these affairs happen on the sly; they never get reported to the other partner. So women must be constant and assertive caretakers of themselves in all sorts of sexual relationships, even the seemingly safe ones.

Remember, both men and women can transmit the AIDS virus and some other sexually transmitted diseases (STDs) without showing any symptoms themselves. You or your partner may not even know you're infected. And statistics reveal a grisly domino effect: AIDS is a gift that goes on giving. Every time you have unprotected intercourse, you're opening yourself to the possibility of contracting the diseases of every partner your partner has ever had.

As a result, the AIDS epidemic is demanding some special dating rituals that are different from those we've been used to since the sexual revolution of the sixties and seventies introduced us to the delights of a freewheeling life-style. Among these are:

- A period of healthy skepticism and information gathering
- Slower moves toward the bedroom
- Insistence on intimacy before intercourse
- A shift toward monogamous, long-term relationships
- Increased acceptance of periodic abstinence and celibacy

These seem like a return to the fifties. Are we suggesting that women step backward into that time of repression and sexism? Certainly not! We're suggesting a mode of operating which is based on sexual pleasure and which is empowering to women, and ultimately to men, too. For in addition to the rituals listed above, there are the following trends:

- Increased assertiveness of women
- Increased mutual responsibility for safe and safer sex

Not only are the rituals changing, new habits are developing. For instance, one of our roving reporters writes from her college campus that it's actually "cool" to carry condoms and that people who don't practice safer sex are considered to be nerds. "Remember how hippies used to put flowers in gun barrels?" she says. "Well, we were sitting around the other day talking about putting condoms on them."

New rituals and habits demand new etiquette—between first-time sexual partners and also between ongoing partners. Of particular concern for women is the age-old question: Exactly what are our rights?

We strongly believe that it's time women gave up the old sexual practice of giving in to men. We believe it's time women adopted a new attitude, time we learned to protect ourselves by knowing the facts and by insisting on safe sexual encounters.

Diane's response is typical of this new brand of know-how:

"If there's anything good about AIDS, it's that it's finally stopped me from sleeping around and made me look at how I'm taking care of myself. It's changed my whole outlook on sex, friendships, everything. It used to be that I just went with whatever other people wanted. Now I have to revamp all my ideas and understand it's OK to play safe. It's OK to ask a man to use condoms—and if he has a problem with it, then maybe I ought to rethink whether I want this relationship to be sexual, or whether I want this relationship at all."

As women like Diane and Betty rethink sex, they can begin to expand the boundaries of their sexuality beyond slam-bam encounters:

- Sex is more than intercourse.

- Safe intercourse is more than condoms.
- And safe sex is surely more than abstinence or unquestioning monogamy.

We believe that safe sex starts with safe relationships between women and their partners. You can consciously choose safety in your sexual relationships. Your ability to make that choice depends on how well you know yourself.

## *Knowing Yourself: The First Step in Opting for Safety*

How do you decide to have sex safely with a new partner?

Imagine setting out to undertake any other kind of major adventure that contains a degree of danger—climbing a mountain or swimming across a lake, for instance. You probably wouldn't begin without knowing a great deal about your own capacities—your strengths, your fears, your attitudes, your skills.

Sex is just that kind of adventure, and it requires the same order of self-knowledge. Before you can know what kinds of sex are going to be safe for you, and certainly before you can begin to trust a partner with your safety, you have to know how to trust yourself. This means you need to understand all aspects of yourself—how you think and how you feel, as well as what kinds of physical sensations turn you on.

Sex isn't something that's just physical or that happens secretly in the dark, disconnected from the rest of your life—even if your style may be to sneak it. Sex is certainly more than intercourse, and even more than genital activity. It's energy, like love or anger or creativity, and this energy is an intimate part of all of you. It flows through all of your thoughts and feelings, whether you're always aware of it or not. What you do sexually affects, and is affected by, everything else you do. At its most ecstatic, women experience sex as a sense of pure love—connection with themselves, with their partners, and with the universe.

But we've been taught somewhere along the line to think of sex as something limited to genitals and breasts, and as separate and distinct from the rest of our lives. In addition, many of us have been taught that sex is dirty. And many of us have experienced sex as a power-play game of control between men and women.

Most of us received some variation of these messages very early in our lives, from our families. We've heard countless women say that these messages were reinforced by their teachers' embarrassment during the sixth grade menstruation movie, and by how adults looked at their budding breasts. We receive further messages every day from the way sex is presented in the media. Consequently, we may have learned to communicate about sex in a way that's different from how we communicate about anything else. We grew up learning to give and receive X-rated messages, with whispers, jokes, innuendos, and sometimes blatant seduction.

Many women (and men, too) learn to disconnect their sexual actions from their emotions and judgment, feeling that what they do in bed can't possibly touch the rest of their lives. Their sexual style may be to jump into bed with anyone as the whim hits and let the chips fall where they may. Or maybe women have been too scared by negative sexual messages to embark on any sexual explorations at all. If your style is either of these, you may be in special danger of finding yourself in sexual situations that are unsafe for you.

For most of us, safe sex begins with rethinking what sex means. Wholly safe encounters involve your whole being, not just your genitals. Once you understand that sex involves affection, aesthetics, sensitivity, humor, and the whole gamut of human emotions, you can find hundreds of perfectly safe ways to express your sexuality without having to give up sensual pleasure and satisfaction.

In chapters that follow, we'll discuss specifics. But here, let's start with the primary element in creating safe sexual encounters: you.

> Knowledge of your whole self is necessary for truly safe encounters.

We see four essentials to the decision-making process for choosing a safe sexual partner and having a safe encounter: self-forgiveness, self-awareness, self-mirroring, and self-esteem.

## Self-Forgiveness

Some of the women who talked with us said they couldn't begin to think creatively about how to incorporate safe sex into their lives until they'd forgiven themselves for certain past sexual behaviors.

If there are incidents in your sexual past that were unsafe, or that you fear were unsafe, you may have leftover feelings about them such as anxiety, anger, sadness, and especially confusion, shame, and guilt. These feelings may prevent you from expressing your sexuality now with full responsibility and pleasure. Moreover, the mind acts on the body, and these feelings can be destructive to your natural immune response, increasing your vulnerability to AIDS and other STDs.

For instance, you may have had unprotected intercourse with a bisexual man or a man who'd received a blood transfusion, encounters that may have seemed perfectly safe at the time but that fill you with qualms now, as you look back on them. Or you may be ashamed of having put yourself (or found yourself) in dangerous situations, maybe involving drugs or alcohol.

The following exercise is designed to help you forgive yourself enough so that you can practice safe sex from now on—with pleasure.

### *Undoing Self-Blame*

Think about what happened to make each encounter unsafe.

Now focus on what *really* happened. Exactly what was your part in the encounter?

Ask yourself the following:

- Were you forced or scared?
- Was there information you didn't know?
- Did you think you needed protection only for birth control?
- Were you operating under the myth that only "natural" sex is satisfying?
- Did you fall for flattery or seduction?
- Were you trying to please your partner?
- Were you looking for love?

If you can answer yes to any of these, you were probably doing exactly what you were conditioned to do by your "good-girl" upbringing, that is, giving in to male superiority. In other words, you may have become a bad girl by being a good girl.

If this description fits you, you don't have to keep giving yourself a double whammy. You can forgive yourself and adopt the attitude that sexual safety starts today. You can learn and practice a new way of having safe encounters.

When you're ready, try this visualization:

On your inhale breath, clearly picture each unsafe incident, one by one, in your mind.

On your exhale breath, picture each incident fading like an old photograph, dissolving into vapor, or fluttering to the ground like a dry leaf (use whatever image feels right to you to disperse the incident).

Finally, picture yourself receiving an award for what you've learned from each unsafe encounter. Really picture the award. If it's a diploma, read what's written on it. If it's a trip to Fiji, take yourself there in your mind—and enjoy the surf!

## Self-Awareness

If you're like most women, focusing on yourself may be difficult for you, and especially difficult during sex. It may seem much more natural to concentrate on what your partner wants than on your own safety and pleasure.

Why is this? First of all, a widespread cultural message has been that women aren't worth as much as men. For most of us, this message starts at birth and never ends. It almost certainly follows many of us into our first sexual relationships, where, as a result, we respond to *his* desires and depend on *him* to show us the way.

That's usually what happens if we're lucky. But some women's initiation into sex is through incest, rape, or other forms of abuse. It's estimated that perhaps half the women in the United States are survivors of some kind of forced sex.[1] For women who are abuse survivors, safe sex may be more than safe encounters; it may include a backup system of therapy and group support.

Without the ability to focus on themselves, many women tend to erase themselves sexually so that they have little or no sensation at all, either emotional or physical.

The kind of focusing on self that we're suggesting here is conscious focus that allows you to fully feel both pleasure and pain so that, among other things, you can make realistic judgments about what you want and about whom you want as a partner. Conscious self-focus also allows you to separate past from present so that you can be in the right relationship with your self. It's the first step in choosing and maintaining a right relationship with a partner.

Let's note here that unconscious focus on self can degenerate into mindless self-absorption and insensitivity to everyone else. Used unconsciously like this, self-focus is a defense against feeling, just as surely as self-erasure is a defense against feeling. And when you can't feel, you're not fully in a position of choice about relationships or sex.

Some women have found that the following affirmation and exercise have helped them become more consciously self-focused.

## *Giving Yourself Strokes*

If the notion of giving yourself strokes makes you break out in a cold sweat, begin by taking several deep, cleansing breaths and letting them all the way out. Then say out loud (whether you believe it or not):

- It's OK to think about myself.
- It's OK to feel.
- It's OK that I find it difficult to think about myself and feel.

Next, try this simple sensory exercise: With one hand, start at the fingertips of your opposite hand and slowly and lightly stroke every part of your body that you can reach. Now stroke what you can reach with your other hand.

Feel what you feel with each stroke, and *whatever it is you feel,* repeat out loud: "I'm entitled to feel this."

Do this exercise in any way that feels right for you personally. Use these directions, or adapt them to fit your own situation. The important thing is that the exercise affirm *you*—as you are.

Some variations on this exercise include stroking yourself with a feather or a piece of fur, silk, or satin. You can scrub your body all over with a brush or loofah while you're showering, treat yourself to an overall lube job with massage oil or body lotion, give yourself a snowball massage after a scalding bath or sauna, or try our all-time favorite, skinny-dipping on a hot August night. Don't forget to say aloud to yourself: "I'm entitled."

For times when it's impossible to be private or naked, you can get some remarkable effects through clothing.

Do some variation of this exercise three times a day for at least three weeks. (We know this amount of reinforcement will produce lasting change, but if you think it's too much for you, make yourself a schedule you'll stick to.)

Keep a journal of any changes in your ability to focus on yourself.

## Self-Mirroring (Directed Self-Image)

We're inundated with cultural messages that tell us how we're supposed to look and act. If we want to attract men, the media suggest that we model ourselves after the cuddly sex kittens we see on television, or at least after the body-building, body-beautiful ones.

But thinner thighs are not likely to promote safe-sex practices. Neither is purring and rubbing up against your partner's ankles, unless you stop at the knees. What's going to help you be assertive about safe sex is the confidence to be yourself.

If you're focused on how you're supposed to be, you may have no clear idea of how you actually come across to others. Some women tell us that when they look in the mirror, they don't know how to assess their own images accurately for themselves. They tend to see themselves perpetually as the way they were told they were by some authority figure in the past—too fat, thin, ugly, fidgety, selfish, loud, inconsequential. With self-images like this, it's no wonder some women refuse to look in the mirror at all.

We've found that a video camera is a valuable tool to help women update their self-images. Seeing yourself live, "on television," can give you a sense of your real power and can also suggest areas in which you might change your behavior to become more effective.

If you don't have access to video equipment or don't feel ready to try it, the following meditation has been helpful for many women (and it can be helpful even if you use video).

### *The Woman in the Mirror*

Imagine yourself looking in a full-length mirror. What do you see? How do you respond to the woman you see? Do you like her or dislike her? Tell her what you feel.

Look at her carefully from head to toe. Take your time. Pause at each part, as if you're seeing it for the very first time. Look at her hair, face, shoulders, arms, hands, breasts, waist, stomach, genitals, hips, thighs, legs, feet. Walk around the mirror and look at each part of her from behind. Notice any scars or birthmarks or other differences that help make her special.

Ask her to tell you one thing she likes about herself and listen attentively to how she answers.

Are there any parts of the woman in the mirror that you especially like? Let yourself enjoy them.

Are there any parts you dislike? Since this is your imagination, you can change anything you want. You can give her naturally curly hair or violet eyes.

Do it! Shazam!

How do you feel about her now? Which changes would you like to keep?

Now step through the looking glass and feel what it's like to be inside her body. Again, you can change what you don't like. Move around. Dance. Sing. Yell. Cry. Stamp. Reach out. Let yourself be the woman in the mirror.

As a way of closing, look in the mirror once again and thank the woman there for having this experience with you. Make a date to get together again and say good-bye for now.

## Self-Esteem

Self-esteem is based on self-awareness and self-image. Because of cultural conditioning and natural personality development, women have learned to nurture others as a primary mode of relationship. And most of us have learned well that our self-worth is determined by how well we take care of our partners, sexually as well as in other ways. Some women report having such low self-esteem that they feel worthless except when they're giving pleasure to their partners.

The result is that we tend to project any feelings of worth we have onto others. How many women do you know who systematically put themselves down while fiercely championing a lover's strength, importance, beauty, wit? This enables these women to shine by reflected light rather than having to take responsibility for generating their own.

Low self-esteem can consistently put you in no-win situations. First, it may make it impossible for you to actively choose partners; instead, you may wait to be chosen. Second, it may make it impossible for you to insist on safer sex. As one woman puts it: "If I'm worthless, my needs aren't really an issue. And besides, how can I be giving pleasure if I'm asking for safety?"

How can you become more positively conscious of your sexuality and yourself? One exercise we routinely advise for women is the Pleasure Mantra, a wordless affirmation of self and sexuality.

### *Pleasure Mantra*

First, settle yourself into a totally comfortable position. This can be lying, sitting, or even standing.

One woman reminds us: "In water it's wonderful." Some women like to practice this mantra in sexual postures, as a rehearsal for doing it later with a partner.

A mantra is a personal meditation you can say or sing to yourself. The Pleasure Mantra is even simpler than that. It's a big sigh of pleasure, with plenty of sound on the exhale. The deeper the sound you make, the deeper you're reaching down into your being.

Take a deep breath and let it out slowly, with noise. (If you're concerned about children in the next room, or paper-thin apartment walls, hold a pillow over your mouth. This will muffle the sound, but you'll still feel the vibration.)

Feel the sound giving you an internal massage as it resonates sensuously from your abdomen to your larynx and curls like steam around the roof of your mouth. One woman we know said she could come to orgasm just by doing the Pleasure Mantra. Another woman said she thought the mantra sounded like the mating call of a humpback whale.

Feel what it's like to breathe this mantra over and over again into each cell of your body, from your hair follicles to your toenails. You can move and stretch your body as creatively as you like while you practice.

Take a few minutes to imagine carrying these feelings with

you into your present relationship, or into one you'd like to begin.

Revamping your attitudes to make sex safe may mean revamping some of your attitudes toward yourself. Sexual pleasure and responsibility begin with you. They begin with how you think and feel about yourself, with how you move and how you breathe.

The bottom line here is that your attitudes about sexual safety depend on your ability to love yourself and take care of yourself. And sexual safety goes beyond self-love. Ultimately it depends on your ability to treat a partner lovingly and on your capacity to be treated lovingly in return.

Each woman's needs are individual. It's our hope that you will learn whatever you personally need to assert positive choices about your sexuality in this age of AIDS, so that you can say yes to pleasure and no to unsafe sex.

## SAFE-SEX ROAD MAP FOR CHAPTER 1: AWARENESS AND SELF-WORTH

In Chapter 1, you've read what other women say about revamping their attitudes so that they can become more aware of their own role in the pleasures and responsibilities of safe sex. This Safe-Sex Road Map is to help you discover more about how *you* feel and what you're doing.

### *Journal Keeping*

Many women find it valuable to keep records of their thoughts and feelings. Some women set this up as a daily diary, finding that writing helps them put their thoughts in order and can even be emotionally cathartic. Other women like to organize material in categories.

Some women don't like to write and prefer to keep records in another form. One woman drew a series of cartoons about her life; another painted gigantic portraits of herself and every partner she'd ever had. Another woman marched into one of our offices with a roll of shelf paper, unrolled it on the rug, and displayed a sprawling "family tree" on which she had charted all her relationships.

Whatever your style, some kind of journal keeping can help you understand more about your sexual feelings and behaviors. Let yourself note particularly:

- Your level of awareness
- Your feelings about your image
- Your feelings about your worth
- What you're doing to know yourself and feel better about yourself

## *Personal Safe-Sex Commitment*

To make my sex life safer, I commit myself to doing the following about my sexual attitudes:

________________________________________

________________________________________

________________________________________

________________________________________

# CHAPTER 2

# *The Right Relationship Is a Safe Relationship*

After self-knowledge, the next concern for women's sexual safety is choosing the right relationship.

We don't believe that having one lifelong partner is the only way to have a safe relationship. In the first place, not all lifelong relationships are safe ones. And second, most women have more than one sexual partner in the course of a lifetime. But we do believe that a mutually loving, trustworthy relationship is by far the most effective safeguard against all sorts of STDs.

How do you decide when you're ready to explore the world of safe sex with a partner—what characteristics do you look for in another person? what sexual history? And how do you assess these—do you have to rely wholly on intuition? How do you recognize whether a relationship is right for you?

Let us note here that for some women the right relationship is with another woman, at least for certain periods in their lives. If this is true for you, we want you to know that aside from specifics about intercourse, most of the guidelines in this book apply to sexual relationships with women as well as to those with men. When we emphasize specific guidelines for sex with men, we do so not to overlook your concerns but to inform the greatest possible number of women about safe-sex techniques.

The fact is, dangers of disease for women are much more present in heterosexual relationships than in lesbian ones. Statistics on sexual transmission of AIDS and other STDs strongly suggest that it is through sexual intercourse with men that these diseases are almost always transmitted to women. Lesbians remain, at this writing, almost free of AIDS, unless they've been infected by blood transfusion, intravenous drug use, or bisexual partners (only two cases of infection have been reported as a result of sexual contact between women).

Opinion about the actual dangers for lesbians varies among physicians and AIDS educators. Some say the risks are minimal; others advise using safe- and safer-sex techniques. In this book, we take the conservative view: Whether a potential partner is a man or a woman, it's important to find out about your partner's history.

## *Questions to Ask Your Potential Partner*

Exactly what questions do you ask? Here are some essentials to ask any partner you're considering having sex with.

- As far as you know, are you free of the AIDS virus?
- Have any of your partners of the last ten years contracted the AIDS virus?
- Have you ever used intravenous drugs or shared a needle?
- Have you had a blood transfusion in the last ten years?
- Will you agree to being tested before we have intercourse?

Of course, there's much, much more information you want to know about a partner before you seriously contemplate a safe sexual encounter. We've included an expanded list of questions in the Safe-Sex Road Map section at the end of this chapter. We urge you to use your own instinct and judgment in addition to this list, and be sure to refer to Chapter 7 for more information about AIDS and other STDs.

Once you've asked the questions, how do you assess your potential partner's history? How much of a risk is it if this person has been bisexual or has had sex with a lot of different partners? What about IV-drug use or blood transfusions? What about physical signs and symptoms: If people look healthy and say they're healthy, is that enough? Are there telltale signs to look for?

And even if you know exactly what to look for, how can you be sure you're getting straight answers? Let's start with one of the most basic concerns of any relationship—honesty.

Many women have asked us: "If he tells me we don't need to practice safe sex because he's never been exposed to AIDS, how can I know he's telling the truth? How can I believe him?"

1. *Don't believe him*—and if you think he's lying to you, stay out of a relationship with him.

or

2. *Believe him*—and if you decide to have intercourse, protect yourself by using a condom and spermicide until you're absolutely sure he's free of the AIDS virus or any other STD.

We could write pages about how the FBI grills its suspects to discover the truth and about signs of fibbing to look out for—dry mouth, sweaty palms, shifty eyes. But such pages would be irrelevant. Sexual safety is not primarily a matter of belief but a matter of your taking responsibility for your own well-being. This may include your insisting that he practice safe sex and also that he have the AIDS antibody test after six months of sexual celibacy.

By the way, if he really won't meet your eyes, you might want to find a way to excuse yourself posthaste and forever from a sexual encounter. Go out to dinner with him or take him to see a movie. But *don't* go to bed with him.

Some women go on to ask: "But suppose he's a nice guy, and he's believable. And suppose I want to believe him?"

Unless you have a crystal ball and can see his entire sexual history, remember what we've said so far, and play it *safe*.

- **S**low down.
- **A**sk questions.
- **F**eel good about yourself.
- **E**xercise your right to safe sex.

**1. Slow down:** There's no rule that says you have to go to bed with somebody as soon as you think of it, even if you're attracted to each other.

Women often base the decision as to when to have sex on a ravenous sexual appetite: "when my hormones are popping," as one woman puts it. This is like going grocery shopping when you're hungry; you end up with a basket full of food you don't really want once you get it home. If this is a problem for you, you can take care of your ravenous hormones by yourself so that you can give your intelligence a chance to enter into your sexual decisions when you're with another person. You can masturbate before a date, just as you can eat lunch before a trip to the supermarket.

**2. Ask questions**—And still more questions. Don't be intimidated. You have a responsibility to find out about this person. It is easier for a woman to contract AIDS from a man than vice versa. His history can affect your future.

> **REMEMBER** Every time you have sex with someone, you're having sex with every partner he's ever had.

**3. Feel good about yourself:** Would he have unprotected sex with a woman he suspected might have the AIDS virus? Your body is the only one you'll ever have, and it belongs to you. Love it. And your *feelings* are just as important as his, too.

4. **Exercise your right to safe sex:** Let him know exactly what you want. As we'll point out in later chapters, this is not only sensible safe-sex practice, it's step one in creating enjoyable, exciting sex.

There's a common worry women have about becoming sexually assertive: "If I ask questions about his background or insist that he wear a condom, isn't that likely to turn him off? Is it pushy to ask him to be tested?"

Whether he gets turned off depends partly on how fragile his ego is—an unpredictable factor and one you can't control. What you *can* control is how you express your assertiveness. Turning your partner off or on also depends in large part on just how you communicate your needs as you go along.

When you first enter a foreign country where you're shaky about the language, it can be valuable to have a pocket phrase book along, one of those handy little guides that spell out instant communication: how to say you've lost your traveler's checks or you need to find a ladies' room.

Here are some phrases for beginners in the new language of sexual assertiveness we must all learn in the age of AIDS. We've presented both tactful phrases and tactless ones, the kind you may shudder about blurting out inadvertently (or in some cases wish you were brave enough to say). We've presented both so you can see at a glance the difference between them. You can use these, or phrases like them, and see what reactions you get—whether, in fact, they turn a partner on, or off.

## A Pocket Phrase Guide to Tactful and Tactless Safe Sex

| *To Turn a Partner On...* | *To Turn a Partner Off...* |
|---|---|
| I'd like to flirt outrageously with you, for hours and hours. | Can't you think of anything but intercourse? |
| Let's spend the evening in the hot tub looking into each other's eyes. | I'll sit in the hot tub with you, but don't you dare try to get me into bed. |

(continued)

**A Pocket Phrase Guide to Tactful and Tactless Safe Sex** (*Continued*)

| *To Turn a Partner On...* | *To Turn a Partner Off...* |
|---|---|
| Let's talk about our favorite techniques for safer sex. | You sound like you've never even heard of safe sex. Where have you been for the last few years? |
| If we could spend more time doing things together, we could get to know each other better. | Can't you think of a more creative place to go than your apartment? |
| Sure, I'm really willing to discuss your point of view. But we need to be clear that we're not going to have intercourse until we agree on exactly how we're going to practice safer sex. | Don't be such a jerk about unprotected intercourse. This is my life you're playing with. |
| It feels good to be able to discuss safer sex practices with you. | If you can't even say the words, how can I trust you in bed? |
| Let's share our AIDS test results. | Waddaya mean you haven't been tested! |

To understand why it's so important to get your language right, let yourself expand your concept of safe sex and put it in a historical context. Safe-sex principles and asserting your sexual rights apply to more than the AIDS epidemic or even other sexually transmitted diseases. Disease is only one kind of sexual danger women face. Sexual relationships can pose all sorts of physical and psychic threats, especially if men and women have limited relationship skills and therefore limited choices.

Throughout recorded history, sexual intercourse has been physically dangerous for women. While it may have brought women much pleasure, it has also brought with it unspeakable risks of repeated pregnancy and childbirth in centuries without reliable contraception, medical care, or anesthesia. Moreover, throughout much of history, and in some cultures still, sexual intercourse has effectively meant slavery for women—once a man had intercourse with a woman, he owned her, just as surely as he owned his farmland or his goats. And for her real or imagined infidelity, punishments could range all the way to death.

The women's movements and the advent of reliable birth control and legal, antiseptic abortion methods have vastly improved the lot of contemporary women. But from birth, we're still subject to all sorts of sexual misunderstanding and abuse, most often from those who are supposed to be our protectors. And we still face the age-old threat of rape; that's why we're taught not to accept candy from strangers or walk outside alone at night.

So women do have a different historical outlook on sex than men. What the AIDS epidemic has done is to put women and men in the same boat. Intercourse is risky for us all now, although statistically it's still more risky for women; that is, in heterosexual relationships, AIDS is most easily transmitted from the man to the woman.

> **HOT TIP** Whether you believe your partner has been exposed to the AIDS virus or not, if you decide to have genital intercourse,
>
> **PROTECT YOURSELF.**
>
> Use condoms and spermicide and practice the other safe sex behaviors outlined in this book.

## *Guidelines for Ongoing Partnerships*

The changing times are exerting stresses on ongoing sexual relationships as well as new ones.

First of all, the social ethic has changed. This is no longer a Victorian era where women are supposed to serve men without questioning. It's not even like the fifties. This is an age of uppity women, where many of us maintain careers in which we've learned how to get ahead in a man's world. It's imperative that women today translate that learning into their ongoing partnerships and acquire the techniques necessary for asserting themselves and making healthy sexual decisions.

Second, the media tell us that reducing the number of sexual partners statistically reduces one's chances of contracting the AIDS virus. Partner hopping and extramarital cheating are becoming less acceptable, and monogamy is resurfacing as the lifestyle of choice. For many Americans, this is a turnabout from the freewheeling sexual mores of the sixties and seventies. Both women and men are having to choose relationships more carefully and having to learn how to live in relationships safely and long-term. This includes learning to enrich sex lives that may have become humdrum over the years.

But AIDS statistics about partner hopping originated from studies of gay men, who may have had hundreds, or even thousands, of sexual encounters, vastly more than most women are likely to have. Studies of infected women are beginning to show that these statistics may be irrelevant to women. Most women who have gotten AIDS through sexual transmission have gotten it from repeated intercourse with one infected partner, not from casual exposure to many partners. This raises the question of safety even for women in long-term relationships. Whether they want to believe it or not, there is a possibility that their partners have had outside affairs in the last ten years and may have been infected with the AIDS virus.

Under the following conditions, an affair may be merely a logistical problem:

- If the affair is known to both partners
- If the affair is acceptable to both partners
- If the partner who has had or is having the affair is willing to practice safer-sex techniques and be tested for the AIDS virus

Most affairs, however, are conducted secretly. And most affairs plunge most couples into deep emotional crises. What do you do if you suspect an affair, or find out about one, or even if your partner tells you outright?

*It's essential that you exercise your right to practice safer sex until you're sure your partner is free of disease.*

You can use a velvet glove technique or an iron fist. What's important is the following:

1. That you discuss the emotional ramifications as well as how to make sex physically safer, and engage a counselor to help if the subject is too painful or difficult for either of you.
2. That your partner be tested if it will set your mind at rest (make sure the test is confidential). Remember that the point here is not to have a power struggle with your partner but to protect yourself from the possibility of contracting a deadly disease, and to safeguard present or future pregnancies.
3. That you practice the safest possible sex until you are absolutely sure.

**REMEMBER** An affair doesn't have to be a current one to put you at risk for AIDS. The incubation period can be as much as ten years or even longer, so any partner your partner had could have transmitted the virus.

What if *you* have an affair?

Exactly the same principles apply to you as to your partner: full discussion, testing, and safer-sex practices.

Fear of AIDS causes some particular stresses on women's relationships:

## Fear-Related Problem No. 1: False Intimacy

When there is instant monogamy, one of the problems women report is the sense of false intimacy, a sense, as one woman puts it, "That we're a couple so we're supposed to be in love. But we're not really in love. We're a couple because we're afraid to play around anymore."

Anita's story is an eloquent example of how false intimacy develops, and ends:

Anita met Larry after they'd both been tested negative for

the AIDS virus. Their attraction was immediate and physical, and on their first date, they spent the night together at her apartment and made unforgettable love. Larry refused to wear a condom. He insisted that the sex was ecstatic because it was "natural." Both Anita and Larry knew that unprotected intercourse with multiple partners is like playing Russian roulette, so with their arms wrapped around each other that next morning, they solemnly vowed that their relationship would remain exclusive.

"But it was terribly premature," explains Anita now. "We didn't even know each other. We leapt into a sexual commitment before we were ready to make an emotional commitment. After a while, we realized we didn't even like each other, but we felt forced to stay together because we'd made this vow. It was kind of like an arranged marriage. We finally had a blowout fight and haven't seen each other since."

## Fear-Related Problem No. 2: Staying in an Abusive Relationship

Another problem women relate is that fear of AIDS keeps them from leaving a long-term relationship even when the relationship ceases to nurture and sustain. This is especially painful for women whose partners abuse them, and it raises particular problems for women who have developed patterns of co-dependency.

Marilyn learned addictive patterns of sexual relating from her family, in which she was repeatedly abused:

"Staying with Frank was just a repeat of how I'd learned to accept abuse when I was growing up. The more he drank and yelled and hit me, the more I imagined he loved me. He used to punch me in the stomach so the bruises wouldn't show, but when he broke my collarbone a friend finally told me, 'That's not love, that's something you talk to a shrink about.'

"And I did talk to a shrink. And I got myself to a women's center, which gave me a lot of support. Women there helped me work out the part I played in staying on and on, and made me question what I was getting out of the relationship.

"I was finally ready to pick up my kids and get out, and all of a sudden AIDS was in every newspaper. I got really scared. I thought, 'The sex is great when he's not drunk, and it's better to stay with Frank than die of AIDS.' I stuck it out for another year and a half. I didn't know what else to do."

> Getting out of an abusive relationship may be more important than sticking to a partner because of fear of AIDS.

Anita and Marilyn are examples of women caught in negative relationships through fear of AIDS, and stuck there through lack of training in how to relate differently. And there are countless women who may be trapped in relationships with infected partners because they are economically dependent on those partners.

But we know of many examples of other women who have risen to the crisis by revamping their sexual attitudes, reframing their fears as a challenge for their own growth. These women have discovered ways to take excellent care of themselves in all kinds of sexual situations, and you can read their stories throughout this book.

## *Meeting the Challenge*

Whether you're in an ongoing partnership or contemplating a new one, there's a key to meeting the special challenges of the age we live in. That key is communication. Communication is an essential part of sex. Remember that T-A-L-K is a four-letter word that means intercourse.

You can use discussion to help develop intimacy and romance with a new partner or a long-term one.

*Talk*...about your sexual feelings. It's OK. After all these centuries of cultural taboo, talking about sex is finally in (that's one of the positive byproducts of the AIDS epidemic). Find out what sex means to both of you.

*Talk*...about what you both like, how and where you like to do it, when, and for how long. Do you like to be slowly tantalized? Closely held? Stroked with velvet? Do you turn into a jungle animal at the midnight gong? Most partners never take the opportunity to talk about what makes them tick sexually. They've been trained to believe that sex is only physical, so they jump right into each other's bodies and neglect each other's minds and emotions.

*Talk*...about what you both *don't* like. Here's a chance to find out if this person has your best interests at heart. If anything about sex is scary for you, this is the time to bring it up. For instance, if you've ever had any kind of abuse, chances are that sex can restimulate feelings of fear and anger. Talking can help you learn whether this is a sexual relationship that's going to work out for you, emotionally and physically. And initial discussions may prevent misunderstandings later if you do become sexual partners.

Here are practical how-to's about three musts for safe communication in relationships that range from casual dating to long-term monogamy: giving clear messages, asking for what you want, and setting boundaries.

## Giving Clear Messages

Personal growth flourishes in an atmosphere of safety. Part of making sex safe is communication. In sex, as in all aspects of relationships, straight communication leads to ultimate health and safety. A friend of ours calls the nonstraight kind "curly communication."

Here are a few communication basics that may help.

## *Communication Don'ts*

- *Don't* interrupt: "Oops! I need to call my hairdresser."
- *Don't* defend: "But last night you said..."
- *Don't* argue: "...And furthermore..."
- *Don't* name-call: "You're so pigheaded about condoms."
- *Don't* lay blame: "If you'd brought the condoms, we wouldn't be in this mess."
- *Don't* take blame: "Oh, I'm so terribly sorry. It's my fault you forgot the condoms. I should have reminded you."
- *Don't* remove praise and appreciation with a big "BUT...": "Thanks for buying all those condoms. BUT whatever possessed you to get so many? They don't keep for more than three years, you know."

## *Communication Do's*

- *Do* use positive "I" statements: "I like it when you tell me what you expect."
- *Do* directly say what your personal tastes and feelings are: "I feel good when you touch me there."
- *Do* appreciate your partner's good points: "Thanks for preparing such a sensuous bath."
- *Do* listen to your partner: "I understand that you forgot the condoms because you don't like to use them."
- *Do* ask for clarification if you don't understand what your partner is saying: "Do you mean you absolutely won't wear condoms, or do you mean you want help making them more sensual?"
- *Do* detach from any curly communications, such as the ones listed above under "don'ts": "I'm aware that just as we started talking about how we could try to make sex safe for

both of us, you started to interrupt (defend, argue, etc.). Let's cool off for a while and then get back together again when you're more able to hear me out."

## Asking for What You Want

Before you can ask clearly for what you want sexually, you have to know what you want. And that's a sticking point for many women. You may have to overcome a lifetime of reinforcement that your desires are not important. Not only that, but remember that for the preceding forty-odd centuries, women have been considered objects, just like household goods, and our sexual desires have not been consistently or wholly taken into consideration.

So the first move is to activate your self-esteem and give yourself permission to have sexual desires.

The next move is to call up crystal-clear images of just what it is you want for yourself sexually. Be careful not to choose activities primarily because they'll please your partner. You're allowing yourself to nurture *you* here.

We consider this "Asking for What You Want" exercise crucial to practicing not only pleasurable sex but safe sex as well. Your partner may not always want to take the trouble for safe encounters, and it's important that you develop techniques for ensuring that they happen.

Once you've figured out what you want sexually from your partner, here's a four-step program for effective asking:

1. **Think of the consequences:** Do you really want what you're asking for—(*total* focus? sex *every* night?) There's an old saying: Beware of what you wish for, because if you visualize it strongly enough, you're almost sure to get it.

2. **Visualize what you want as distinctly as possible:** If what you want, for instance, is that your partner pay attention to other parts of your body as well as to your genitals, take time several times a day to imagine this

occurring in exactly the ways you'd like. Let yourself be explicit, and enjoy the visualization.

If you have trouble visualizing, know that this is normal for women who don't have a Ph.D. in Asking. Keep trying.

If images of anger, fear, or sadness come up instead of images of pleasure, acknowledge that these feelings are present and real. Then let them go, and let yourself get on with the pleasure.

Some women encounter problems letting go of these feelings. If this occurs for you, try this: Each time you inhale, visualize clearly what makes you angry or scared or sad. And then each time you exhale, imagine that image dissolving into a healing vapor. One woman said she imagined so much mist that she felt like an extra in *Brigadoon*.

If you have feelings that won't dissolve easily, that's a clue that you need to pay attention to those feelings and work on yourself, your relationship, or both. Don't just stuff the feelings down and decide never again to try to visualize what you want. If you can't visualize what you want for fear of raising negative feelings, your safe-sex potential is being seriously diminished.

3. **Say what you DO want, not what you DON'T want:** If you want your partner to stimulate you a certain way, be direct. Say: "I'd like you to rake my sides hotly with your fingers." Don't say: "I wish just once in a while you'd think about touching me somewhere besides my breasts."

   Your partner's likely to remember *whatever* you say and even interpret what you say as a command, especially if he or she is anxious to please you. If you keep repeating what you don't want, that's what you're most likely to get.

4. **Start small:** Begin by asking for what you know your partner can give you; try not to ask for Mission Impossible. You can always add items to the agenda once you've had a few successes together.

## Setting Boundaries

What if he won't play safe? What if he doesn't want to practice safer sex, or doesn't feel it's necessary, despite all your reasonable and sexy communications?

One of the ways to maintain health is to understand what your personal boundaries are and to be able to set limits when necessary—for instance, having unprotected sex with strangers or using drugs as a companion to sex. Being able to draw a firm bottom line means strength and self-respect, not pathological rigidity or so-called frigidity.

Knowing how to establish and maintain boundaries is important when sex doesn't feel safe and you need to keep a relationship from becoming sexual. It's also important when your partner has a powerful personality so that you can keep yourself from being bulldozed in all sorts of negotiations.

### *How to Say No*

A client tells us about visiting her sister in Spain some years back:

"We couldn't walk down the street without being followed by groups of men who always seemed to be hanging out on the corner. They were loud and intrusive, and I was annoyed and scared. I tried everything I knew to ward them off. I ignored them, I begged them to go away, and finally I just shouted No!, figuring that was universal enough language so they'd get the message. But they only laughed uproariously and followed us even more noisily.

"My sister pointed out that in Madrid 'No' actually meant 'Yes,' especially when it came from a not-too-badly-put-together American woman. 'If you want a man to believe you mean No, you have to begin way up here (she pitched her voice at screech level) and not let up until you run out of breath.' With this, she turned on our followers and scattered them with an operatic string of No-No-No-No-No-No's worthy of a famous diva."

We tell this story, because, ridiculous as it seems, this is how women sometimes have to say no to unsafe sex.

There are men, who, for whatever their reason, refuse to

take no for an answer: "He insisted on pushing himself on me, even though we'd just met," Marnie told us, "and I didn't know what to do. I didn't want to hurt him. But I didn't want unprotected sex with him. In fact, I didn't want sex with him at all. So I literally pushed him away and left the scene. Now I'm trying to deal with the guilt: If a man wants sex with me should I have sex with him even if I'm not interested?"

The answer to Marnie's question is *No. No,* so you can hear it in Madrid. *No* in thirteen languages, if you have to.

What if he tries to guilt-trip you with comments like: "I was just trying to be friendly" or "You led me on" or "The problem with you is you're frigid."

Be aware that remarks like these are probably a result of his emotional fallout and most likely have nothing to do with you. They certainly don't show consideration for your pleasure or safety.

*It's essential that you remove yourself from any sexual situation that you don't want or that feels unsafe.* In order to do this, you may have to wrench yourself away from two forms of training that are embedded in the brain wrinkles of many women brought up in this culture:

1. That it's your job to have sex with anyone who wants to have sex with you, or at least feel flattered by the request (*Not true*)

2. That guilt trips and accusations are aimed at you because, in fact, it's you who've done something wrong (*Not true*)

**REMEMBER** There's no law of the land that says you have to be a people-pleaser beyond the limits of your physical, emotional, and spiritual safety. That means it's OK for you to say No to any sex you don't want, even if it may hurt someone else's feelings. And if polite language doesn't get immediate results, it's OK to up the decibel level until he gets the message, that is, until he changes his behavior and backs off.

## *What if I Suspect I Have AIDS?*

Responsibility for safe sex means not only protecting yourself, but also protecting your partners. Besides, if you're going to insist that your partners are free of infection, it's only fair that you be sure you're free of infection yourself.

> Whether your partner is a man or a woman, you have a responsibility to think of your partner's well-being as well as your own. Make sure you are HIV-negative before you start a new sexual relationship or continue having unprotected intercourse in an ongoing relationship.

If you think you're showing symptoms of any STDs (see chart in Chapter 7), or if you think there's even the remotest possibility that you might have been exposed to the AIDS virus within the last ten years:

1. Practice only the safest sex techniques.

2. See your physician. It's important to find a physician who is informed about AIDS and other STDs. Believe it or not, some are still misinformed. And your physician's attitudes are crucial, too. AIDS is a scary business, and skepticism or moral posturing is not going to be helpful for you. If you feel comfortable with your physician, you'll be more likely to ask questions and get answers you can make sense of.

3. If you and/or your physician think you might have the AIDS virus or be in a high-risk category for acquiring the virus, get tested. See the section on testing in Chapter 7. Make sure your test is absolutely confidential. Make sure you have pre-test and post-test counseling—and you might want to have other counseling as well. Think about whether or not to submit the charge for testing to your insurance company. Reports say that some insurance companies are

refusing to continue to insure women and men who have the AIDS antibody test, whether the test results are positive or negative.

**4.** If you have a confirmed diagnosis for the AIDS virus or any other STD, inform your present partner and any other partners you think you might have infected over the years. Difficult as this is, you have an obligation to let these people know so that they can figure out what to do about their own health care. They also have an obligation to let *their* partners know, and to be tested and to practice safer sex. Get any support and help you need for this task.

*Until there is an effective vaccine or a cure, this kind of personal responsibility is the only way to keep AIDS from spreading.*

## *Denial of AIDS: "It'll Never Happen to Me"*

AIDS is changing our patterns of sexuality and our patterns of dating, courtship, cohabitation, and marriage. But there are still millions of women and men who don't want to believe there's an AIDS epidemic and who stand fast in denial—denial that AIDS could ever affect them.

Denial is not a matter of stupidity, or even necessarily of bullheadedness. It's usually an understandable response to a seemingly impossible situation. It's a defense mechanism that enables you to keep on functioning even in disaster. It's the kind of emotional response that children develop to survive growing up with alcoholic or abusive parents, and the kind of physical response that allows you to snowshoe through a blizzard with a broken leg to find milk for the baby.

Denial of AIDS has elements of all of the above, and it takes a great deal of education and support to break through it to the kind of acceptance that enables you to change your attitudes and behavior.

## If Your Partner Is in Denial:

1. Go especially slow.
2. Be absolutely clear and firm about your own needs for communication, commitment, testing, condoms and spermicide, and/or other practices you feel will make sex as safe as possible for you.
3. Get support from friends, from professionals, from responsible media coverage of AIDS. Affirm and reaffirm your right to insist on personal safety.
4. Detach yourself from his arguments against going slow and practicing safe sex. Be assertive enough to detach yourself from him if he won't respect your point of view and allow you to practice safe sex while you're with him.
5. *Finally, if he won't play safe, activate your self-esteem and leave him. When you next decide to seek out a partner, look for one who has respect for your needs and a realistic view of the world.*

## SAFE-SEX ROAD MAP FOR CHAPTER 2: SAFE RELATIONSHIPS

In Chapter 2, you've read what other women say about initiating and maintaining safe relationships. This Safe-Sex Road Map is to help you discover more about how *you* feel and what you're doing.

## *Twenty Questions for a Safe Partner*

Getting to know a potential partner thoroughly is one of the musts for ensuring a safe sexual encounter, and here's your chance to ask all the questions you ever wanted to ask.

We suggest that every woman play Twenty Questions before making the decision to engage in any physical sex play with a partner. But don't feel you have to limit your questions to twenty. You're at liberty to ask as many as you wish. And to equalize the relationship, you can encourage your potential partner to ask you questions, too.

Be aware that any one of these questions can spark a discussion, or an argument, and how these go will also help you determine how safe this relationship is going to be.

Before you start firing away at one another, you might want to think about just what it is you want to find out, and of course this will vary from partner to partner. But the bottom line is: Is this person free of the AIDS virus, and is this person willing to practice safe sex? If the answer to either of these questions is No, or causes you doubt, find another partner to have sex with.

1. Do you know how AIDS is spread?

2. Did you ever do IV drugs?

3. Did you ever share a needle?

4. Did you ever have intercourse with anyone who did IV drugs or shared a needle?

5. Have you had a blood transfusion in the last ten years?

6. Have you had intercourse with anyone who had a transfusion in the last ten years?

7. Have you had sex in the last ten years with a gay or bisexual man?

8. How many sex partners have you had in the last ten years?
9. Do you know whether these former partners are free of the AIDS virus?
10. Are you willing to be tested?
11. Are you willing to spend time getting to know each other before we have physical sex?
12. Do you think sex is just physical, or do you believe emotional feelings are important in a sexual experience?
13. What's your idea of a thoroughly romantic evening?
14. Do you believe that love is necessary for great sex?
15. If you could have sexual satisfaction any way you wanted, what would that be?
16. How would you feel about giving that same level of satisfaction to a partner?
17. What kind of condoms do you like best?
18. Do you enjoy giving massages?
19. What's the most creative safe-sex technique you can think of?
20. Do you think women are as important as men?

## *Relationship Progress Chart*

Keep tabs on your safe-sex assertiveness by jotting down how you're handling your sexual encounters. To organize this, head up separate pieces of paper with:

- Clear Messages

- Asking for What I Want
- Setting Boundaries

As you add your experiences to these lists, include your thoughts on the following:

- My limits are:
- This is what I want in a sexual relationship: (rank order the list)
- This is whom I want it from:
- This is what I can give myself:
- Three ways I can ask for each item on the list:

## *Ad for a Lover*

Now's your chance to write an ad for a personal column, without having to mail it and deal with the responses. Compose an ad for a lover, for someone to share safe sex with you, as well as other aspects of your life that you consider to be important.

Be explicit about the qualities this person must possess to apply for the job. Is deepness of soul a requisite for you, or do you prefer great legs? You can ask for both. You can ask for whatever you want; this is your ad. Also, you can write as many ads as you want, to express different parts of your personality.

As you write, be sure to include exactly the kinds of activities you'd like this person to enjoy safely with you. Clearly outline your feelings about romance, commitment, intimacy.

And be sure to let prospective readers of this ad know something about you, and just exactly how you intend to show your appreciation to the person who meets your description.

"Ad for a Lover" is especially effective when used in groups. We've tried it with up to twenty-five people, both same-sex and coed. We shuffle the ads so they're anonymous, and everyone reads them out loud around the room (of course, advertisers can decide whether they want their ads to be shared).

The cumulative effect is always touching and funny and wise. Everybody has a chance to hear what kinds of things are important in different relationships, and to expand their safe-sex repertoires.

## *Personal Safe-Sex Commitment*

To make my sex life safer, I commit myself to doing the following about the way I choose partners or relate to my ongoing partner:

________________________________________

________________________________________

________________________________________

________________________________________

# CHAPTER 3

## *Safe Sex Turns Women On: Options Other than Intercourse*

In this age of AIDS, once you make the decision to be sexual with a partner, what exactly can you safely do in bed?

For starters, you can try activities other than intercourse. Call them foreplay, or petting, or even teasing: They mean *not going all the way*. The problem with all these names is that they imply that genital intercourse is "the real thing" and that anything else is only a preamble. Furthermore, they imply that touching anything other than the genitals isn't even close.

In naming new behaviors for a new sexual age, we prefer to reframe our whole view of sex rather than suggest a series of activities that may be seen as warm-up exercises. In searching for what to call experiences of sex beyond the genitals, we like the name "extragenital" (X-G for short). But the name we like best is "outercourse."

We know that sex without intercourse is safe and that sex without genital involvement is especially safe. But is X-G sex real sex? Can outercourse turn women and men on? Can it satisfy? Clients and colleagues have told us emphatically, Yes!

This chapter is based on a research study about women's responses to extragenital stimulation, sexual touch that doesn't dive straight for the homing sites, like the clitoris and vagina.[1] Although the women who chose to be in this study considered themselves easily orgasmic, the findings may help you think in some new ways about your own homing sites, and beyond. What the findings say to us is that there are dozens of ways to look at sex other than the old performance trip that says it's got to include the genitals or it isn't sex.

The common belief is that the key to all women's sexual excitement is sandwiched somewhere between clitoris and G spot, but the women interviewed in the study repeatedly answered that, much as they enjoyed having their genitals stimulated, they experienced much of their sexual pleasure in areas of the body beyond the vulva.

Their extragenital pleasures were centered in places you might not think of as particularly sexy as well as places that leap easily to mind, like lips and nipples. These women mentioned every part of their bodies, literally from head to toe—fingers and eyelids and ears, and even elbows and knees. More than half the women interviewed were actually able to come to orgasm without having their genitals stimulated at all.

We don't cite the experiences of these women in order to set yet another sexual goal for you to strive for. We cite them because they tell us something important about safe sex for women: *"Safe" can be both erotic and satisfying, and safe sex is natural and intuitive for women.*

The findings tell us that when women experiment, women may find many other forms of sex as enjoyable as intercourse or even genital stimulation. Many women report that extragenital stimulation is even more enjoyable. This is not astounding news. We suspect that women have known this all along, although they may not have known it consciously or been able or willing to verbalize it.

For one thing, sexual creativity is a hard thing to bear in mind, let alone communicate to your partner, when you're trapped in the missionary position. For another, women have been so conditioned for so many generations to take care of men that we may not know how else to behave.

What about the men in our sexual lives?

In reframing our ideas of a sexuality that's both safe and pleasurable, women need first of all to understand themselves; if their sexual lives include men, they also need a basic understanding of how *men* have been conditioned over the generations.

Women need to understand that a sexual encounter may involve more for men than either safety or pleasure. The goal of sex for men is often intercourse, because successful intercourse—that is, thrusting, with ejaculation within the vagina—has historically meant proof of "potency." In other words, intercourse can be a power symbol, the ultimate proof of manhood.

When our male partners get turned on, they may be pushing for proof positive each and every time, whether they're aware of it or not, and they may become quite anxious if they have to stop short of "success."

So although outercourse may be a safe and satisfying sexual answer for many women (and our educated guess is, for many men, too), there's been a cultural barrier to its widespread practice.

## *Touching for Safety: What, Where, and How*

Exactly how do you do outercourse? A forty-three-year-old friend of ours who's newly single voices the following complaint: "I was raised believing that sex means doing one thing, and one thing only. What do you do if you don't just jump into having intercourse? And what do I tell my daughter?"

One fact about outercourse that may be helpful for you to know is that the largest organ of pleasure is the skin. There's literally no place on the skin that doesn't have erotic potential. Stroking any area, massaging it, nuzzling, and nibbling, even pinching and spanking, can all be sexual experiences for women—complete and satisfying, even if we skip the genitals altogether.

Of course, different folks respond to different strokes. The skin has memories, which are stored in the brain, and particular memories are activated by certain kinds of touch on certain places. These are often very individual and conjure up very personal images. For instance, women have talked about how holding hands brings back scenes of innocence and little-girlhood and how back rubs and facial massage re-stimulate deep feelings of being nurtured. These feelings may lack exact words because they may pre-date words, they may spring all the way from infancy, when every need was taken care of by doting parents.

"A full-body hug? The pleasure is sweetened by the longing," comments Marie, now a mother herself. "I know that the hugging and holding and all-over patting I give my babies was what I got myself when I was tiny, and there's always a part of me that yearns to go back there—to when I was loved so unconditionally and so completely physically. At this level, there's really no separation between physical and emotional."

> **WARNING** Not all sexual sensation is pleasure.

Body memories can work both ways. If a woman has been abused or raped, her brain retains memories of those incidents, even if her cognitive mind has forgotten about them as a circuit-breaker mechanism of self-protection. Present stimulation, even if it's entirely noncoercive and loving, can reactivate terrifying memories from the past. The result can sometimes be a torrent of tears or anger that has been stored for years.

While anger or tears may seem like inappropriate responses to tender touch, it's important to understand that this kind of release is normal. It not only may help resolve old pain but also help open up blocked pathways to pleasure.

If this kind of release should occur while you're making love, don't try to stop it. Let it continue until it plays itself out naturally, and discuss the feelings with your partner as soon as you're able. Part of thoroughly safe sex is the emotional freedom to be fully expressive and yet still unconditionally accepted.

## Massage

Massaging each other is a wonderful way to have a safe and loving sensual relationship. In fact, says Karen, a masseuse and acupuncturist: "Massage is making love without sex."

She tells the old Japanese tale of Yuriko, who hated her sister-in-law and wished to murder her. Yuriko consulted the wise woman at the top of the hill, who gave these instructions: "Massage your sister-in-law each afternoon, and then put two of these drops in her tea."

After several weeks, Yuriko returned to the wise woman: "I want to bring these drops back to you because a new situation has developed: I don't hate my sister-in-law anymore; I love her."

The wise woman smiled and responded: "The drops are only colored water, and harmless. But you do not need to kill your sister-in-law any more, so your problem is successfully solved. You see, it is impossible to massage someone every day without learning to love them."

So if you get a chance to massage your lover or be massaged, enjoy it. You don't have to be a professional. And, yes, it's all right if you already love the person before you begin the massage.

While this story about Yuriko makes a point, there's a further point we'd like to make: Like all aspects of sex, touching and massage communicate feelings. Yuriko was lucky that her hate didn't pour through her hands onto her sister-in-law, for it well might have.

Before you begin to touch your partner, it's important to know what feelings you want to communicate, and to prepare your hands to deliver that communication. Some women say it's helpful to meditate on exactly what they want their touch to say and to visualize it flowing through their fingers.

The flip side of this discussion of touch communication concerns when *you're* the one on the receiving end of a massage or any other kind of touch that's supposed to be pleasurable. If you should feel anger or anxiety or demand flowing from your partner's hands, remember that you can stop the process and ask to talk about the feelings. Your partner may be unaware of what's being communicated and may be able to literally re-think things so that you get a wonderfully loving and relaxing massage.

**REMEMBER** You don't have to endure touch that doesn't feel good or appropriate to you. In fact, you can make it your responsibility to see that you get what *does* feel good.

## Creating Sensation

Not all extragenital touch needs to be as formal as massage. How many other ways of touching are there? Too many to count.

For starters, you might like to know just where on your body you like to be touched and also what kinds of touch excite you. In the Safe-Sex Road Map section at the end of this chapter is a Personal Extragenital Matrix, with directions, so that you can chart exactly what's erotic for *you*.

We want to emphasize here that extragenital sensation is a completely individual matter. No woman feels that *every* part of her body is erotic—although some woman say that under certain conditions it may feel that way. If you don't like having your earlobes nibbled, that doesn't mean you're a prude. And there's no rule that says you're abnormal if your nipples happen to feel like radio dials when your partner twirls them.

This brings us to another important factor about outercourse. The kind of touch is as important as where on your body your partner touches you. Most women who've talked with us agree with the old Elvis lyric, "Love me tender..." According to reports we've heard, slow and tender touch is an almost universal turn-on for women. But some women want more forceful kinds of touch at different times; squeezing, pinching, and spanking can feel as erotic as stroking, patting, and nuzzling.

> "There are a hundred ways to create sensations by manipulating the flesh. You can tickle her, massage her...hold her and even hang on to her, knead and stroke and explore."[2]

You can also receive a great deal of pleasure from giving extragenital pleasure to your partner if you stop to feel the sensations in your own body. One woman tells us that one of the most pleasurable things she can do for *herself* is to stroke her lover's torso with the inside of her forearm: "The insides of my arms are particularly sensitive, so when I lie beside my partner I can draw my arm over that beautiful human body and think of silk or velvet or rose petals. I breathe into the feelings and let them radiate all the way through me."

And other women speak of simultaneous pleasure: "One of our favorites is tantalizing each other's sides and backs very lightly and slowly with our fingertips, all the way from our buttocks to our shoulders. The trick is to keep going, slowly and inexorably, no matter how excited you get."

## What about Kissing?

Although kissing is extragenital behavior, it does involve the exchange of body fluids. The Centers for Disease Control reports that exchange of saliva is not as dangerous as exchanging blood and semen because the AIDS virus is less concentrated in saliva and because saliva is not as hospitable an environment for the virus. AIDS educators tell us that it would take several quarts of saliva to produce a dangerous amount of the AIDS virus. However, because deep kissing may present some risk, we cannot recommend it as an absolutely safe sexual activity.

Barbara gives us a positive, safe-sex perspective on how to deal with the desire to kiss: "One of my all-time favorite activities is kissing. I could kiss all day and all night. In fact, I always wanted to enter a kiss marathon—I'd be a shoe-in.

"Of course AIDS has cut short a prize-winning kissing career, but I find I can still get a lot of mileage out of *nuzzling and sucking*—that full, expanded feeling in my mouth and lips. I ask my partner to turn over (so we don't accidentally start kissing) and I find places that feel really good for me to nuzzle. Fingers are great, and the back of the neck—and ears are fantastic.

"And it's a two-way street. My partner loves it, and I get all sorts of encouragement to go on and on."

## *Safe-Sex Effectiveness Training: A Note for Your Partner*

As a woman's partner, you can be a model student and memorize all her sensitive highways and byways. But intellectual grasp won't make you a great lover. Mutual satisfaction is determined by your attitudes and your approach, and how these coincide with her feelings of the moment. Here are four musts:

1. **Get permission:** Notice both the verbal and nonverbal cues. If you move in on her aggressively or against her will, you may lose her trust. Women can experience violation in all parts of their bodies, not just in the genitals.

2. **Move slowly and tenderly, at least at first:** Sex is one area where strength and speed aren't a special advantage. Don't simonize her like your car.

3. **Pay attention to her:** This is not the time to go over the baseball standings or the Dow-Jones average in your head. One woman complained that her husband used to keep his eyes glued to the television set while he was caressing her. Not only did she finally leave him, she developed an undying distaste for the late late show.

4. **Take some of your cues from her:** See if you can fit into her rhythm. Try breathing at her pace, moving at her speed. Making love is a dance you do *together*.

## *Creative Outercourse*

Extragenital sex doesn't have to be confined to the bedroom, or even necessarily to touching your partner. It can mean any kind of sexual play that concentrates on aspects of the relationship other than each other's genitals. Women tell us that role-playing and romance, even picking up the phone, can turn into creative ways to participate in totally safe sex, and women say that working on their techniques can be an outright pleasure.

Here are stories from women we've met.

## Especially for Ongoing Relationships

### *Sneaky Safe*

(From LouAnn, a long-time wife, who found herself bored with "plain old sex-on-the-rocks.")

"We'd been married sixteen years and were just beginning to face our sexual blahs when AIDS hit the news, so any fleeting little thoughts we had of having affairs or opening up our marriage went out the window.

"After three kids and running a business together, we'd learned to solve problems, so we decided to see what we could generate all by ourselves.

"First, we tried to remember when sex had been hottest for us, which was before we got married, when we were sneaking around and keeping our hands above the belt. We reminisced about some favorite old haunts, like the backseat of his father's Buick. When we thought about it, we realized the anticipation had actually been more exciting than the sex when we finally did go all the way.

"So we set out to be teenagers again. This time around, we had to sneak away from our children, not our parents. And we made a rule that we couldn't have intercourse. Instead, we began kissing and petting, and we discovered dozens of ways to play with each other all over—most of them above the belt."

## Especially for New Relationships

### *Romance: Tripping the Light Fantastic*

(From Daphne, newly returned to the dating scene, who decided with her potential partner that the way to deal with the several-month waiting period for their antibody test results was to have a romantic interlude rather than a physical one.)

"We knew we weren't going to have intercourse. And we didn't want to "mess around," as we used to call it when we were teenagers, so we decided we could go all the way in other ways. Romance wasn't a preamble to anything during that period. Romance was *it*.

"We started with lots of eye contact, the kind that says, 'I could just gobble you up'—but we didn't gobble each other. We flirted outrageously across crowded rooms and elevators and little restaurants.

"We sent gifts and wrote charming letters (remember letters?). We affirmed each other in ways I've dreamed about since I was eighteen. I still carry one of his poems in my wallet.

"And we danced. We found a dance studio run by an old Hollywood extra named Mr. D., who loved us and taught us how to waltz and disco and tango. Then we went out to clubs and used up a tremendous amount of energy on the dance floor, and I suspect that we were just as physical and even almost as orgasmic as if we'd been having intercourse."

## For Any Relationship

### *The Phone Phantom*

(From Joyce, who explained that phone sex is tremendously erotic for her—she was referring to consensual behavior here, not dial-a-porn or illegal, harassing, or obscene calls. She described her five-year phone relationship with a man she's decided not to have physical sex with.)

"I call him my phantom lover. Sometimes we touch ourselves and tell each other exactly what we're doing. Over the years, I've learned to work the phone, so I describe what's happening in sultry tones and use pregnant silences and little moans and fast breathing while I imagine the effect on him.

"I sometimes get off on reading him sexy stories. I also like to leave teasing messages on his answering machine when I know he's the only one who's going to pick up.

"He likes to share his fantasies with me in living color. His voice is deep and fine, and when he flirts on the other end of the phone, it sends shivers up my spine. Sometimes he calls when he knows I'm about to go to work and makes me grin all day by laying out the most graphic details of exactly what he'd like to be doing with me."

## How Do I Turn My Partner On to Outercourse?

Men have sensuous feelings all over their bodies, too, and they can also be imaginative about sex. But one of the problems women report is that most of the men they know tend to be goal-oriented and may not be able to see beyond intercourse. If your partner seems to be obsessed with intercourse, you may well be able to teach him other routes to sexual pleasure.

How can women turn men on to outercourse? To find out some surefire techniques, we interviewed several professionals who specialize in exactly that.

These professionals are called partner surrogates, and they work in conjunction with sex therapists to teach clients new ways to express their sexuality, training them directly in rehearsal sessions set up like actual encounters with a partner. In particular, surrogates have training that enables them to teach men to discover the pleasure potential in all parts of their bodies. Some of their clients have physical disabilities that prevent them from having genital sex, so extragenital training is especially important.

In any event, part of what most surrogates explain to their clients is that there will be no genital contact at first. Therefore, the men they work with are not expecting genital touch and may be more open to relaxing into pleasurable sensuality, being less goal-oriented, and enjoying it more.

### *Patricia's Bubblebath Caper*

(From Patricia, a professional partner surrogate who has advised us throughout this book on the specifics of how women and men can have safe and pleasurable sexual encounters.[3] One of Patricia's favorite ways to teach a man about extragenital pleasure is to give him a bubble bath. This way, he learns to focus on the sensations all over his body instead of concentrating on his penis and how he's supposed to perform magic with it.)

"Yes," Patricia agrees, "Giving him a bubble bath *is* serving him. But that's different from being subservient. Remember, the purpose of this exercise is to get his focus off his penis—and besides, the next bubble bath will be for *you*.

"First of all," she tells us, "Transform the bathroom into a nonthreatening, delightful environment. Appeal to all his senses. Light some candles to cast a soft, reassuring glow. Play soothing music. Burn pleasant incense. Prepare a tub full of sweet-smelling bubbles and invite him to disrobe and enter it, like an honored guest.

"Kneel by the tub. Pluck up a handful of steamy bubbles and let him watch you play with it. Invite him to breathe deeply and relax into the warm water.

"Now begin to stroke him with the bubbles on your hands, every part of him you can reach except the genitals. Start slowly and gently with his face and ears, sliding your bubbly hands over him and rinsing him off as you go along. Make slippery circles on his neck, shoulders, chest, arms, and hands. Now move to his feet and toes, up to his knees and thighs, and then up to his stomach and chest again. Keep this up for as long as half an hour, and ask him to be aware of how his body is feeling.

"Then invite him to step out of the tub, and dry him off with big, fluffy towels. Ask him to lie on his stomach so you can enjoy playing with his back just as you've played with the front of his body in the water. Slowly and gently touch his hair, his arms, his back and buttocks, his thighs, calves and feet. Don't try to work out stiff muscles here, he can get that at the health club. This is just gentle stroking to make him aware that he has pleasurable sensations in every inch of his body. Make sure he's breathing fully. If he holds his breath, that means he's stopping himself from feeling.

"The next move is to lie with him and cuddle face to face, or back to front in spoon position. While you're cuddling, make sure you don't fondle his genitals and that you don't have any goals of further touching or talking. Just breathe together.

"After a while, ask him to share with you how his body is feeling and what he felt in different areas as you bathed or stroked him."

Patricia says that most of the men for whom she'd been a partner surrogate not only had been unaware of the pleasure potential all over their bodies but had never experienced what it is like to pleasure a woman without feeling they had to perform genitally.

She stresses that a most important part two of this bubble bath technique is that your partner give you the royal treatment the next time—again, with *no* genital contact and *no* goal of intercourse or orgasm. This gives him an opportunity to feel what it's like to give sensuous pleasure to you without any of the expected sexual feedback. For many men, it's frankly a blessed relief. And your partner may find he has such a good time undemandingly giving you pleasure that it becomes a habit.

Here are some other ideas about how to entice your partner into safe-sex outercourse play and discovery, and, for comparison, some ideas that are practically guaranteed to turn your partner off:

### A Pocket Phrase Guide to Initiating Outercourse

| *To Turn a Partner On...* | *To Turn a Partner Off...* |
|---|---|
| Let's see how many places feel good without touching our genitals. | Don't touch me *there*—you know that's off limits. |
| Let's see how we respond when we play Toe-69 and suck on each other's big toes. | You're such a Johnny One Note. Can't you think of any other place to touch? |
| If I promise to lie perfectly still, will you promise to run your silky fingertips all over my body...? | If you cared about me, you'd know where I like to be touched. |

*(continued)*

**A Pocket Phrase Guide to Initiating Outercourse** (*Continued*)

| *To Turn a Partner On...* | *To Turn a Partner Off...* |
|---|---|
| Let's see if I can lubricate or you can get hard if we tango with our raincoats on. | When did you last take a shower? |

## *What's "Normal"?*

Women who've talked with us say they're able to experience sexual pleasure all over their bodies, from head to toe. We've presented some of their positive responses to extragenital stimulation in the hope that you'll let go of inhibitions and experiment. This way you can treat yourself and your partner to some new sexual options in an age where the media increasingly tell us: Sex is dangerous, and therefore all sexual pleasure is dangerous; wrap yourself in rubber or stay celibate.

But please don't take the idea of outercourse as yet another sexual norm you have to follow slavishly. The point of this chapter is to encourage you to feel better about yourself sexually and to take more control of your sex life. We don't want you to feel bad about yourself just because you don't come every time you brush your hair.

> "It has always been my contention that the only 'should' about sex is that...it should be fun."[4]

Let's take a look at our sexual norms and try to put women's extragenital sexual experiences into some kind of perspective that may be useful to you.

In the first place, sexual tastes and preferences vary widely from person to person and even from time to time. Not everyone is turned on by the same things all the time.

Second, there's no such thing as unconditional sexual pleasure. All pleasures have their conditions, and these also vary from person to person and from time to time.

Let's explain this: Imagine you feel a blissful loss of control during a sexual experience. Your bliss doesn't exist in a vacuum. Many elements play their part, and these elements include not only you but your partner as well. Your mutual expectations certainly affect your pleasure, as do factors such as timing, privacy, and comfort. Also essential are your immediate emotional states, your relationship to your partner, and the phase of relationship you're in (are you just falling in love or have you been married for sixteen years?). Clearly, your age and health are important, along with what's going on in your lives beyond the sex. If you've got a big paper due, or are working two jobs, or just moved the family from Boston to Kansas City, you probably don't have much energy left for sexual experimentation.

In fact, when you stop to think about it, the quality of pleasure you enjoy is affected to some degree by just about everything that's going on in your life. And when you stop to think about that, it means you can exercise quite a bit of control over whether sex is going to be fun for you. You can recognize optimum conditions, and sometimes you can even create them.

> **HOT TIP** If orgasm helps you be more sensitive to extragenital stimulation, and if you need genital stimulation for your orgasm, you can first masturbate yourself to orgasm and then play at safe outercourse with your partner for as long as you want (see Chapter 5 for tips on "flying solo").

In the last hundred years, since sex research officially began, it's been impossible for scientists to articulate a definitive sexual norm for women. Even women sexologists struggle with this. So don't ever let a partner get away with telling you that what turns you on is abnormal.

Even though we can't responsibly deliver an exact sexual norm, we can tell you that there are four common threads that run through all the stories we've heard:

1. Each woman is turned on by doing sexually what feels good to her.

2. Each woman has a very personal definition of sexual satisfaction.

3. Each woman is an active participant in the sexual encounters that satisfy her (be aware that her imagination and her will can be active even though she may choose to keep her body quite still).

4. Each woman feels profoundly connected with herself and her partner during the sexual encounters that satisfy her.

## SAFE-SEX ROAD MAP FOR CHAPTER 3: YOUR EXTRAGENITAL SENSITIVITY

In Chapter 3, you've read what other women say about extragenital stimulation and pleasure. This Safe-Sex Road Map is to help you discover more about how *you* feel, and why. Sex is more than just intercourse or just homing in on the genitals. It's possible for women to enjoy intense sexual feelings all over their bodies and to come to orgasm through extragenital play. And this way, as far as we know, women are at zero risk of contracting the AIDS virus.

Exactly where, beyond the genitals, are women sensitive? During an interview, one woman exclaimed: "I don't know where on my body I'm *not* orgasmic. I need to be mapped!" Women in this chapter talked about all parts of their bodies and about various kinds of touch, by hand, mouth, and full body. Look for the categories they mentioned in the Extragenital Matrix at the end of this section. You may want to add some categories of your own.

## *Making Your Personal Map*

You'll need a pencil or other drawing materials and paper (as large as you have on hand).

### Part I

Let's begin with relaxation.

First, take a deep breath and let it all the way out. Keep doing this until you feel loose and flowing, like a silk scarf.

Next, close your eyes and let yourself remember a peak sexual experience you've had, a time that was pleasurable from beginning to end, a time when you felt a constellation of feelings you could call sexual ecstasy. It can be recently or long ago. Let yourself feel it now as if you were there.

What are the images that reappear? What are the feelings? Remember how open you felt at that time, or how passionate or safe or elated. Or remember the strength and tenderness of those moments, or the smells, or the way the light played across your partner's body, or the radiant expression on your partner's face.

Remember your whole body, all of you, not just the few inches that make up your genital area. Now, breathe into your whole body—fingers and toes and earlobes and breasts—each of the parts you remember being aware of during that experience.

Remember the kinds of touch that made your body smile.

Stay there for as long as you like, and when you're ready, go on to Parts II and III.

### Part II

This is a chance for chart mavens to play. (If charts and numbers are a turnoff for you, skip this and go on to Part III.)

Look at the Extragenital Matrix at the end of this Safe-Sex Road Map: thirty-six parts of the body and fifteen kinds of touch, with room for personal additions. Using a 1 to 10 scale (10 for ecstasy), translate your own peak sexual experience onto the chart on pages 62 and 63. For instance, your hair being stroked might rate a 6, while your toes being nuzzled gets a 9. Go through the body list thoroughly and lusciously. You may surprise yourself at how important the rest of your body is when you stop to consider it.

Note that you can repeat this chart for other sexual experiences, and you can use negative numbers to show where and how you did not like being touched.

## Part III

This is a more right-brain version of Part II.

With your eyes closed, draw a picture of yourself enjoying that remembered time of sexual ecstasy. Be as outrageous or lyrical as you like. Don't worry about artistic ability or realism. That's one of the reasons you have your eyes closed.

Open your eyes and see yourself on paper. You may want to fiddle with your portrait to make sure it has all the pieces you need for the rest of this exercise.

To make your extragenital awareness map, use a 1-to-10 scale (10 for ecstasy) and jot numbers all over your picture until you look like a paint-by-numbers still life. Note that you can repeat this exercise for other sexual experiences, and you can use negative numbers, too, to denote where you did not like being touched.

Some women prefer to tattoo their body maps with descriptive words or phrases instead of numbers. One woman flatly refused to use numbers. She said it reminded her of math class and her hours of humiliation at the blackboard with Miss Algernon, the dragon of Franklin High. This woman adorned her portrait with colors—red for Most Hot, then orange, yellow, green—the whole spectrum. She said she felt like a rainbow when she finished.

However you decide to map yourself, be acutely aware of how you feel when you finish, and write it down.

*Mapping yourself for extragenital pleasure or orgasm will help you remember that there are sexual options other than intercourse. These options are perfectly safe, and they can be both erotic and satisfying.*

## ***Personal Safe-Sex Commitment***

To make my sex life safer, I commit myself to doing the following about discovering options for outercourse:

________________________________________

________________________________________

________________________________________

________________________________________

## Your Personal

| | *Kind of Touch* | | | | | | | |
|---|---|---|---|---|---|---|---|---|
| | *Touching by Hand* | | | | | | | |
| **Where on My Body** | **Stroking** | **Patting** | **Rubbing** | **Squeezing** | **Pinching** | **Spanking** | **Other** | **Sucking** |
| **Head and Face** | | | | | | | | |
| Scalp | | | | | | | | |
| Hair | | | | | | | | |
| Cheeks | | | | | | | | |
| Eyes | | | | | | | | |
| Nose | | | | | | | | |
| Lips | | | | | | | | |
| Tongue | | | | | | | | |
| Ears | | | | | | | | |
| Behind ears | | | | | | | | |
| Earlobes | | | | | | | | |
| **Neck and Torso** | | | | | | | | |
| Neck | | | | | | | | |
| Throat | | | | | | | | |
| Shoulders | | | | | | | | |
| Breasts | | | | | | | | |
| Nipples | | | | | | | | |
| Armpits | | | | | | | | |
| Ribs | | | | | | | | |
| Stomach | | | | | | | | |
| Abdomen | | | | | | | | |
| Upper back | | | | | | | | |
| Lower back | | | | | | | | |
| Buttocks | | | | | | | | |
| **Arms and Hands** | | | | | | | | |
| Upper arms | | | | | | | | |
| Lower arms | | | | | | | | |
| Elbows | | | | | | | | |
| Wrists | | | | | | | | |
| Palms | | | | | | | | |
| Fingers | | | | | | | | |
| **Legs and Feet** | | | | | | | | |
| Outer thighs | | | | | | | | |
| Inner thighs | | | | | | | | |
| Knees | | | | | | | | |
| Behind knees | | | | | | | | |
| Ankles | | | | | | | | |
| Feet | | | | | | | | |
| Toes | | | | | | | | |
| **Full Body** | | | | | | | | |
| **Other** | | | | | | | | |

## Extragenital Matrix *(See directions on page 60.)*

| *Kind of Touch* | | | | | | | | | |
|---|---|---|---|---|---|---|---|---|---|
| *Touching by Mouth* | | | | | | *Touching with Other Parts* | | | |
| **Nuzzling** | **Licking** | **Fluttering** | **Blowing** | **Nipping** | **Other** | **Hugging** | **Full-body** | **Hair massage** | **Other** |
| | | | | | | | | | |
| | | | | | | | | | |
| | | | | | | | | | |
| | | | | | | | | | |
| | | | | | | | | | |
| | | | | | | | | | |
| | | | | | | | | | |
| | | | | | | | | | |
| | | | | | | | | | |
| | | | | | | | | | |
| | | | | | | | | | |
| | | | | | | | | | |
| | | | | | | | | | |
| | | | | | | | | | |
| | | | | | | | | | |
| | | | | | | | | | |
| | | | | | | | | | |
| | | | | | | | | | |
| | | | | | | | | | |
| | | | | | | | | | |
| | | | | | | | | | |
| | | | | | | | | | |
| | | | | | | | | | |
| | | | | | | | | | |
| | | | | | | | | | |
| | | | | | | | | | |
| | | | | | | | | | |
| | | | | | | | | | |
| | | | | | | | | | |
| | | | | | | | | | |
| | | | | | | | | | |
| | | | | | | | | | |
| | | | | | | | | | |
| | | | | | | | | | |
| | | | | | | | | | |
| | | | | | | | | | |
| | | | | | | | | | |
| | | | | | | | | | |
| | | | | | | | | | |
| | | | | | | | | | |

# CHAPTER 4

## *The Latex Factor: Doing It, Talking about It, and Liking It*

If you've been reading safe-sex pamphlets and listening to talk shows about condoms, dental dams, and latex gloves, you may begin to envision your preparations for sex as turning you into a frogwoman dressed for a deep dive.

Our purpose in this chapter is not to wrap you in latex and send you on your way but rather to offer you the most comprehensive information about how to protect yourself if you choose to have sexual intercourse with a partner who may be at risk, and about how to protect your partner if you are at risk.

With all the media coverage and the books about AIDS that seem to spring up daily, what more could there possibly be to know about the latex factor in safer sex?

For starters, the slogan "just use condoms" has received the major emphasis in the prevention of transmission of AIDS and other STDs. But there's a big difference between slogans and education. Slogans don't deal with the emotional element so crucial to women's sexual satisfaction. And they omit the simple truth that most women and men who started being sexually active since the advent of the pill in the early 1960s don't know how to use condoms and are embarrassed to ask.

Women are socialized to be caretakers; not surprisingly, the burden is on us, not only to buy condoms for men to use but also to persuade men to use them.

This chapter offers specific information about how women can deal assertively and positively with the ins and outs of condoms as well as diaphragms, latex gloves, dental dams, spermicides, and other diving gear designed to make sexual encounters safer.

## *Shopping for Condoms*

Public statements against birth control may cause some people to wonder if condoms are legal and openly available.

Yes, they are! You don't need a doctor's prescription to buy condoms, and if you're a minor, you don't need a note from your parents. (In 1977, the Supreme Court ruled that no state may bar minors from purchasing condoms without parental consent.)

Condoms are cheap, usually about 50 cents each. And they're easy to buy in most areas. You'll probably find them at the checkout counter of your drugstore or supermarket, and you may also find them in convenience and discount stores.

If you have trouble finding condoms, look for "prophylactics," the more formal name. They come in a variety of over 100 types and brands, in different shapes, textures, and colors, lubricated or unlubricated. To attract women, who buy 40 percent of all condoms,[1] one manufacturer has begun to market condoms in simulated leather cases to carry in a purse.

Some people find the selection delightful, but if you're new to buying condoms, you may find it overwhelming. Deciding what type, brand, and quantity to buy and having to ask the person behind the counter about them, often in the presence of others, can be unnerving, especially for adolescents. Almost half the male high-school students in one study said their embarrassment would actually prevent them from purchasing condoms.[2]

A friend who works in a drugstore reports that even though condoms are openly displayed there, groups of teenage boys sometimes come in together and circle the display until one gets up the nerve to buy. If you're embarrassed about buying condoms, you might start by looking in a big, impersonal chain store. Pick out a couple of different brands of three to a package and purchase them with other items you need.

Alternatively, you can get condoms from vending machines; for instance, many colleges are putting them in locker rooms and dormitory bathrooms. You can also get them from mail-order houses (see Chapter 9 for the names of some).

Your local family-planning or STD clinic may also stock condoms, and they may be considerably cheaper there, if not free. You might also be offered counseling in how to use them. This counseling is usually offered free or at nominal cost.

> **WARNING** Condoms are not foolproof, even though they are factory tested. So even if you do everything right, you're still playing Russian roulette if you have intercourse with a partner who has the AIDS virus.

Here are some guidelines to help you choose condoms that will provide maximum protection against STDs, including AIDS:

- All condoms are stretchable, so one size pretty much fits all.
- Use only latex condoms (see the section later in this chapter on "how condoms work").
- Use only condoms that are not outdated (check expiration date on the outer package).
- Be sure the package contains instructions about removing the condom from the wrapper and about how to use the condom.
- Look for condoms with receptacle tips instead of rounded ends. These have a space at the end to catch the ejaculate; this makes the condom less likely to leak, slip off, or break.
- Lubricated condoms should contain nonoxynol-9, at least 5 percent.
- *Candy condoms and ticklers are not prophylactics and do not provide protection against the transmission of*

*body fluids. They should not be used for safer-sex practices.*

To determine which ones you like best, you'll have to take them home and experiment; beyond the safety factor, it's a matter of personal preference. Some are ribbed or studded, supposedly to increase a woman's enjoyment, but few women we know report added vaginal sensation from the ribs or studs. Some men report greater sensations with lubricated condoms that contain gels or spermicidal jelly. Other men swear by condoms that contain a "delaying cream," which numbs the penis and helps retard ejaculation. This can provide more staying power for men who don't have control over when they ejaculate, but it can also numb the vagina and decrease vaginal sensations.

Some condom hazards: Dyes in colored condoms may run, but most are stable. Allergic reactions may be caused by certain brands, especially those that are scented or lubricated.

If one kind of condom is irritating to you or your partner, try another. Experiment with the whole gamut until you find your favorites.

# *Twelve Steps to Safer Condom Use*

## Buying and Storing Condoms

**1.** Be sure that all condoms are individually sealed in air-tight wrappers.

**2.** Keep condoms in a convenient place, wherever they're easy for you to use every time you have sexual intercourse. Our friend Lissa keeps an assortment in a handwoven basket beside her bed so she can offer her partner a choice.

**3.** If you plan to store condoms for more than a few days, be sure they're in a relatively cool, dry place. Stored properly, they should keep for about three years.

Heat and cold can deteriorate latex. So don't keep condoms in your purse or the glove compartment of your car for long periods, where they may be exposed to extreme temperatures.

If the latex material of the condom is sticky, brittle, or obviously damaged, *do not use it.*

## Opening and Testing Condoms

**4.** Open the package very carefully. Tearing into it in the heat of passion can damage the condom. It's a good idea to experiment with a number of different brands to see which ones open most easily for you.

Students at the first annual condom-rating contest sponsored by the Stanford University AIDS Education Project voted the Gold Circle Coin Type "Best Overall" and "Easiest to Use." Several students praised the brand for its foil wrapping that can be opened with one hand.

**5.** You may want to test-drive condoms to see how far they'll stretch. You can blow them up like birthday balloons or fill them with water. Try different kinds, and be sure to play with them until they break so you know just how much stress they can withstand (lubricated condoms are tougher than unlubricated ones).

*Then throw them away! Once you have stretched or inflated condoms, do not use them with a partner.* It may reassure you to know that you will not be the first to test your condoms. They have been electronically pre-tested during manufacture. For example, each Trojan is put on a stainless steel form and dipped into an electrically charged water bath that can detect even microscopic holes. Faulty ones are automatically rejected from the assembly line.

Be aware, however, that as of this writing, there are no mandatory quality-control requirements for condoms, which need conform only to standards voluntarily set by the condom industry itself. One manufacturer reports that federal quality control was never an issue so long as condoms were used only to prevent unwanted conception. The AIDS epidemic, he says, is making the FDA look at condoms much more thoroughly than when their only function was contraception.[3]

## Lubrication

**6.** You may need to add lubrication to the outside of the condom or to the vagina, because latex is dry and the condom can stick or tear. There are many kinds of lubrication on the market, and for protection against the AIDS virus and other STDs, make sure the one you choose contains *at least 5 percent nonoxynol-9*. This is the ingredient in spermicides that kills sperm on contact.

Adding nonoxynol-9 spermicide inside the tip of a lubricated or unlubricated condom can help inactivate the AIDS virus, even if the condom should accidentally break. We'll say more about nonoxynol-9 (N-9) later in this chapter.

Always use water-soluble lubrication (see the chart below), never oil-based lubricants, because they cause condoms to deteriorate quickly, acquire holes, and break.

**Lubricants for Use with Condoms**

| *Do Use Water-Soluble Lubricants* | *Don't Use Oil-Based Lubricants* |
|---|---|
| K-Y Jelly | Vaseline |
| Astroglide | Baby oil |
| Delfen | Cold cream |
| ForPlay | Crisco |
| Lubafax | Mineral oil |
| Probe | Massage oil |
| Ramses | Vegetable oil |
| Slip | Albolene |

To learn how oil-based lubricants play havoc with your condoms, try this exercise taught us by a peer counselor at a local college: Stretch a condom over your hand and open the fingers. Now smear Vaseline (or whatever) on the stretched latex, and watch the condom melt like your nylon panty hose in a bonfire.

Experiment until you find the lubricant that feels, smells and tastes best to you. You may be adding lubricant a number of times throughout each sexual experience, so keep it handy.

**HOT TIP** Even the best water-soluble lubricants can dry out during use. If adding more lubricant seems too messy, you can add a little water instead. Keep a squeeze bottle, squirt gun, or bowl of warm water nearby so that if the lubricant on your latex begins to dry out you can freshen it.

## Putting Them On

**7.** Now for the real challenge: putting the condom on. You can do this as a partner exercise, or either of you can do it alone. Be inventive. We'll offer a few suggestions in the section on eroticizing latex.

First of all, carefully remove the rolled condom from the package.

If there's a receptacle tip, gently press the air out of it before putting the condom on, because air bubbles can cause breakage. You can solve the air problem by using a small amount of water-soluble lubricant in the tip. But be sure you use just a dab, because too much will cause the condom to loosen with intercourse.

If your partner is uncircumcised, pull back the foreskin before putting the condom on.

Roll the condom onto the penis (like putting on stockings). If the condom has a plain end, you'll need to leave about half an inch free at the tip to catch the ejaculate, otherwise, ejaculate may seep up over the rim of the condom and defeat the whole purpose.

Roll the condom all the way to the base of the penis. If the penis is soft, be sure to keep rolling the condom onto it as it hardens, until the entire erect penis is covered. (See the section on eroticizing latex for stimulating ways to roll a condom onto a soft penis.)

Eliminate any air bubbles with a smooth motion outside the condom from tip to base.

If the condom does not fit completely to the base of your partner's erect penis, he should be careful not to insert his penis into your vagina any farther than the condom reaches; otherwise, the condom could slip off.

**8.** Use a large amount of water-soluble lubricant that contains nonoxynol-9 on the outside of the condom and in the vagina before intercourse. If you're too dry, the condom can pull off or even tear.

Your vagina may become irritated when you first use condoms. If this happens, use more lubrication or change your brand.

Use ample lubrication for anal intercourse, too. But remember that anal intercourse is the riskiest of all sexual behaviors.

**9.** Put the condom on *as you begin* sex play. If you wait until you're ready for penetration, it may be too late. Drops of semen may ooze from the uncovered penis before ejaculation, and even one drop is enough to spread infection (and make you pregnant).

*Use a new condom each and every time you have vaginal or anal intercourse. And use another new condom if you have oral sex after genital or anal intercourse.*

## Keeping Them On

**10.** It may be necessary to hold onto the base of the condom to keep it from slipping off during intercourse, which can happen if your vaginal opening is very tight or if the penis is getting soft.

It can also happen in the course of certain intercourse positions. For instance, when you're sitting on top of your partner, your vaginal lips can grasp the condom in a moment of ecstasy and lift it right off his penis. While this is a tribute to

*Putting a condom on a flaccid penis*

*Putting a condom on an erect penis*

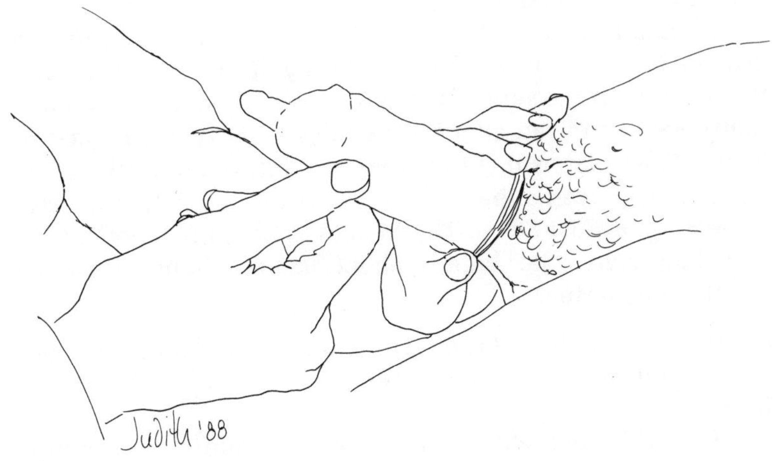


*Rolling a condom to the base of a penis*

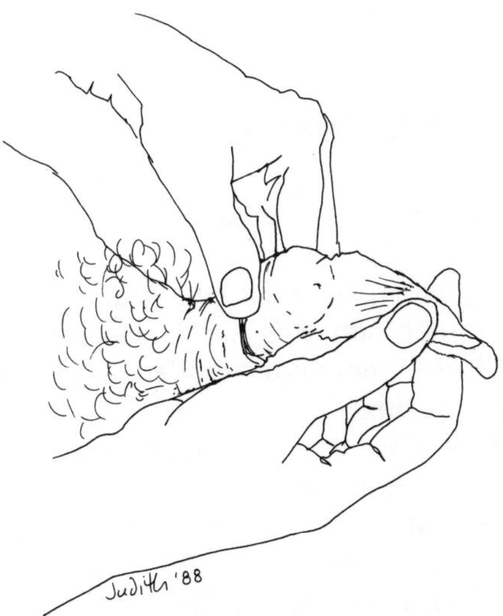


*Pinching a condom during its removal to retain fluid in the tip*

the strength of your vaginal muscles, it may also make for a very unsafe encounter.

A condom called Mentor comes with a safety seal that is designed to prevent accidental slipping during use by sealing the condom to the skin of the penis. The manufacturer claims that it stays on even after the loss of an erection. The manufacturer also claims that the safety seal forms a watertight barrier which prevents the exchange of body fluids, giving extra protection against STDs. The Mentor condom is more expensive than many other brands, about $2.50 each, but it may be worth considering.

**11.** After ejaculation, you or your partner should hold the condom around the base of the penis to avoid spilling the ejaculate.

He should then withdraw extremely carefully and gently.

*He should refrain from thrusting after ejaculation because when the condom is lubricated inside with seminal fluid, it can slip off the penis.* We know this may be a lot to ask, both for your partner and for you, but we feel it's essential for your safety.

## Removing and Disposing

**12.** Your partner should very carefully remove the condom, and wash his penis immediately with soap and water or prepackaged antiseptic wipes. Don't help him remove the condom, because if his semen contains the AIDS virus, you could become infected if it enters your bloodstream—through a hangnail or cut on your finger, for instance.

Discard the used condom. Never, under any circumstances, use a condom more than once.

Never move from vagina to anus or from anus to vagina without changing condoms first.

A tip on throwing condoms away: Condoms may be devilish to get rid of once and for all. Do you remember as a child running to Mommy with those teensy dead balloons you found washed up on the beach? We wonder what archaeologists in the year 4000 will imagine our culture used them for.

If you flush them down the toilet, they may not even reach the beach. Chances are, they'll fill with air and keep popping back up to haunt you or lodge in your septic system and snarl up the works. To avoid having to call the plumber, wrap used condoms in tissue and throw them in the trash.

## How Condoms Work against STDs

We've been talking about using condoms, but how do they help prevent the spread of STDs?

First of all, they're not foolproof. We want to stress that using condoms is not a guarantee that you won't become infected with the AIDS virus, any more than it's a guarantee that you won't get pregnant. Short of celibacy, monogamy with an uninfected partner, or sexual practices that involve no contact with the body fluids of another person, no sex can be guaranteed to be absolutely safe.

But condoms are more than theoretically effective against AIDS and most other STDs.

How do they work? In 1985, researchers at the University of California in San Francisco conducted a test by filling condoms with a fluid containing the AIDS virus. This study demonstrated that condom material blocks the passage of the AIDS virus.[4]

Condoms have also been shown to help stop genital transmission of candidiasis (yeast infections), gonorrhea, and syphilis, and block the passage of the bacteria that cause chlamydia and the virus that causes herpes.

Be aware, though, that condoms offer protection only to the penis and to whatever the covered penis touches. Herpes and syphilis lesions, which can transmit disease, also occur on parts of the body not covered by condoms.

A word about "natural," or lambskin, condoms: They are made from the lining of sheep intestine, which is a naturally uneven membrane. The condoms may have thin-walled portions or even microscopic holes that allow the tiny bacteria and viruses of the STDs to pass through. Lambskin condoms are more effective at preventing conception than at preventing STDs because sperm are much larger than the viruses and bacteria that cause STDs; thus sperm can't pass through the membrane.

Although some men prefer the feel of lambskin condoms, we do not recommend them. Only latex condoms are recommended for protection from STDs.

## *Why Condoms* Don't *Work*

*Condoms don't work if they aren't used each time you have sexual intercourse.* Research estimates that 10 percent of condom failures occur because they're not used properly or consistently.

> Use condoms every time. You can contract STDs any time you have intercourse with an infected partner.

The ten most common reasons given for not using condoms are:

- People don't think they really work.
- They think their partners are not infected.
- They think they, themselves, are not infected.
- They think condoms take the fun and spontaneity out of sex.
- They're afraid the man will lose his erection.
- They forget to carry them.
- They don't know how to buy them.
- They're too embarrassed to bring up the subject.
- They're afraid of offending their partners.

- They're too drunk or high on drugs to put on a condom, or even to remember whether they've worn one.

Maybe you've heard a few more excuses you could add to this list.

*Condoms don't work if they're not used properly.* They can leak, break, or come off during intercourse.

They usually leak or break if they're old, if they've been exposed to heat or sunlight, or if they've been handled roughly. They also can break if an oil-based lubricant has been used on them.

They can come off accidentally if you don't follow the steps outlined above.

*If a condom should break or come off during vaginal intercourse, do not douche, because this can spread infection. Instead, immediately insert additional spermicide containing 5 percent or more of nonoxynol-9.*

# *Other Protection against STDs*

## Nonoxynol-9

Nonoxynol-9 (N-9) is a mild detergent that is an ingredient in most spermicidal jellies and creams and in the lubricants of some condoms.

In laboratory studies, N-9 and some other related detergents have been found to be highly effective in destroying a wide variety of STDs on contact. For maximum benefit, it should remain in the vagina for four to five hours after intercourse, and women are advised not to douche. (When used for contraception in conjunction with a diaphragm, both diaphragm and spermicidal jelly or cream must remain in place for six to eight hours after intercourse.)

But don't use N-9 as your only safer-sex protection. It must be used *in addition* to a condom.

Imperfect as it may be, a spermicide with at least 5 percent

N-9 properly used, in conjunction with a condom, offers the most complete barrier to STDs available at this writing.

Since the safety and effectiveness of N-9 for anal use has not been demonstrated, we cannot positively recommend its use in anal intercourse.

Noting that spermicides are sometimes swallowed during oral sex, the Centers for Disease Control reports that N-9 is low in toxicity—that is, it's safe if ingested in small quantities.

Ingesting N-9 conjures up a variety of images for women: "Suppose my 4-year-old uses my spermicide as toothpaste?" says one. Another says: "Suppose my 16-year-old thinks she can swallow it to keep from getting pregnant or getting AIDS?"

In answer to these questions: *N-9 kills sperm and the AIDS virus on contact, not systemically;* it won't work if you swallow it. But it won't kill *you* if you swallow it, either, though we suggest you keep it out of the reach of your 4-year-old. We also suggest you give your 16-year-old specific and factual information about spermicides and STDs.

## Foams, Jellies, Creams

Foams, jellies, and creams are barrier contraceptives. Laboratory experiments have shown that when they contain at least 5 percent N-9, they kill the AIDS virus and most other organisms that cause STDs.

Foam coats the vaginal lining, and so it may be more effective than jellies or creams. They are all designed for use with condoms and diaphragms, however, and we do not recommend that you use them by themselves, either for birth control or for protection against STDs.

## Diaphragms

A diaphragm is a barrier that covers the cervix, and it is usually identified as a contraceptive—to prevent sperm from passing into the uterus and beyond. By blocking the cervix, it also helps prevent viruses and bacteria from entering the uterus and keeps them from infecting the blood supply by that route. The diaphragm must be used with a cream or jelly containing at least 5 percent nonoxynol-9 and should be used in addition to a condom. This way, it becomes a more effective barrier both to sperm and to the organisms that carry disease. The diaphragm will not prevent viruses and bacteria from entering your blood supply through tears in your vaginal walls, nor will it protect your partner from infection by you. A solution to this may be a new condom that fits into the vagina and covers the external vulva. As of this writing, this woman's condom is being tested in Europe.

## Dental Dams

Dental dams, or oral dams, are six-inch squares of latex used during dental procedures to create a barrier between the dentist and your blood and saliva, which contain viruses and bacteria.

They can also be used in oral sex as a shield to prevent the passage of STDs from vagina to mouth or from mouth to vagina. As of this writing, there have been no reported cases of AIDS being transmitted via oral sex; however, there have been many reports of gonorrhea and herpes being transmitted by oral-genital contact.

Despite the name, you don't necessarily put them in your mouth for oral sex. Most people who use them put them over the vulva and in the vagina instead. This way, they work as a woman's equivalent of a condom for cunnilingus, to block the exchange of both saliva and vaginal secretions. They can also be used to cover the anus for oral-anal stimulation. Some safer-sex pamphlets recommend that dams be used routinely, just like condoms, if you're not sure of your partner, or yourself.

Dental dams can be purchased in some drugstores and in medical supply stores (see the Yellow Pages for those in your community). Some come lightly scented and in different colors.

In a pinch, people have used plastic wrap as a substitute for a latex dental dam. The problem with plastic wrap is its unreliability as a barrier. It crinkles and may slide around or tear.

## *How to Use Dental Dams*

**1.** Wash and dry them before use. Most of the users who talked with us prefer to wash them because they taste better afterward.

**2.** Cover the entire anus or vulva with the dam, holding two edges firmly with your hands and using your mouth and tongue to stimulate your partner. This takes a little getting used to, but it *can* be done, and can even be fun (see some interesting things to do with dams in the section on eroticizing latex).

Remember, the vulva is more than just the clitoris or the vagina. Make sure the dam covers every bit of the vulva, including clitoris, lips, and vagina.

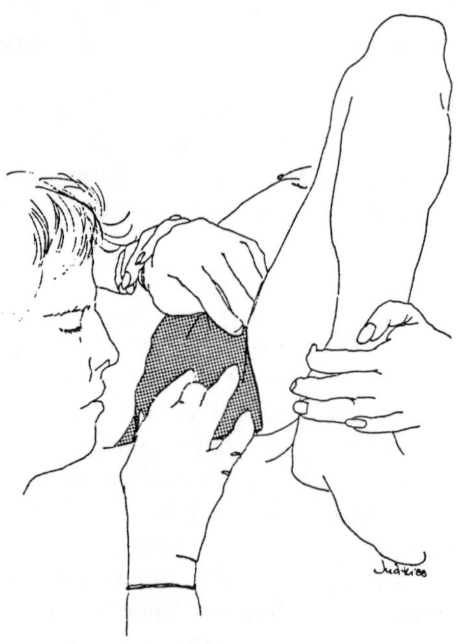

*Using latex gloves and a dental dam*

3. Use a dental dam only once. Observe the same precautions as with condoms: Never reuse, never share, never go from partner to partner, or from anus to vagina, or from vagina to anus using the same dam.

## Latex Gloves

Latex examination gloves are suggested when you use your fingers to stimulate a partner's penis, vulva, or anus. Gloves keep fingernails from accidentally tearing the sensitive tissue in these places, which might invite transmission of the AIDS virus. They also protect these places from coming into contact with a partner's blood supply via hangnails or cuts on the fingers.

Latex gloves are not yet a fashion item, but they are becoming available in different sizes and colors. They can be purchased in most drugstores. (If you feel you need an excuse to buy them, you can say you're painting your bedroom.)

As with condoms, for lubrication use a spermicide that contains at least 5 percent N-9. And use only a water-soluble lubricant, as oil-based lubrication will damage the latex.

## Household Items

There are ordinary household items that can create an effective barrier or kill the AIDS virus on contact. Soap and hot water, hydrogen peroxide, ordinary rubbing alcohol, or diluted household bleach (1 part bleach to 9 parts water) are excellent for cleaning sex toys or other items that may have come in contact with body fluids. Be sure you rinse your sex toys after cleaning them.

Some prepackaged wipes contain N-9, alcohol, and benzylkonium chloride, and are excellent for helping to take off condoms and for cleaning up after intercourse.

## *How to Talk about Using Latex*

So far, this chapter has read rather like a quartermaster's manual: Just have the right equipment at the ready, and you will be disease-free. But we don't want to give the impression that you can make yourself or your partner immune to AIDS and other STDs by covering up in enough latex. Dress like Frogwoman if that's what you choose, but don't count on it as your only commitment to making sex safer.

Technology in itself is just not enough for safer sex. Women have to be able to communicate with their partners. And a major difficulty that women report about using any paraphernalia to make sex safer is getting their partners to agree to use it.

One reason for this may be that since the Pill, sexual responsibility for birth control has shifted almost entirely to women, and men have gotten out of the habit. Also, the effectiveness of antibiotic treatment for most STDs has made these diseases less frightening and so has made condom use less important for protection.

We're a nation out of practice. The prerequisites for safer sex, such as talking about condoms and other equipment with a potential partner, may be simply unknown to many people, especially teenagers.

Women may also have personal roadblocks to communicating effectively about sexual safety. Women we asked named these roadblocks as the most common ones:

- Inexperience in taking care of their own bodies
- Low self-esteem—doubting they're worth the bother
- Lack of self-assertiveness
- Fear of asking a man to take responsibility
- Assumption that condoms reduce men's physical sensations

How do you bring up the subject of making your sexual encounters safe? Here are some ideas:

- You may want to begin talking about AIDS or safer sex in general before talking about your own behavior.
- You may want to talk about your concerns to a friend before you risk conversation with a partner.
- You can role-play with a friend, or even in front of the mirror.

When you bring up your personal safe-sex concerns for the first time with a partner, you could say something like:

"I've been hearing a lot about AIDS lately and I'd like to know more about it. I know it's not easy to talk about this, but from what I've heard, most people don't understand the risks. They don't realize that you can get AIDS even if you aren't gay or an addict. Even a person who shot drugs a few times or had one same-sex experience in high school might be at risk of being HIV-positive. What are your concerns about AIDS?"

As the relationship progresses, you might say something like this:

"I've had to think about whether I've had any risks in my life. I don't think so, but rather than take any chances, I'm willing to use condoms and foam. I couldn't live with myself knowing I wasn't careful about myself and about you."

The following samples of suggested responses may be helpful in situations where your partner is resistant to using safer-sex practices.[5]

| *When Your Partner Says...* | *You Can Say...* |
|---|---|
| I can't feel anything when I wear a condom; it's like taking a shower in a raincoat. | There may be some loss of sensation, but there is still plenty left. |
| I'll lose my erection by the time I stop and put it on. | I'll help you put it on. If you hold and stimulate the base of your penis as I put it on, you'll have extra sensations from the two of us. |

*(continued)*

| *When Your Partner Says...* | *You Can Say...* |
| --- | --- |
| It's so messy and smells funny. | This way we'll both be safer, and no one will have to sleep in the wet spot. |
| I'm a virgin. | I'm not. So let's both be sensible and safer. |
| Condoms are unnatural, fake, and a total turnoff. | So's an infection. So let's give condoms a try. |
| Let's do it this once, and we'll talk about condoms next time. | Once is all it takes. |
| I don't have a condom with me. | I do. |
| Do you always carry a condom around with you, or were you planning to seduce me? | I never leave home without one because I care about myself and I care about us. |
| A condom takes away from spontaneity. | So does death! |
| Latex tastes awful! | Don't worry, we'll try honey or syrup on top. |
| I've never used one before. | Well, then we can learn together. |
| I'm willing to take my chances. | I'm not! I don't want that responsibility. |

Communicating about latex is not limited to heterosexual interactions. As we've indicated in Chapter 2, lesbians also may have to be concerned. The AIDS virus has been found not only in semen, but also in menstrual blood, and, to a much lesser degree, in saliva and vaginal secretions. Therefore it's theoretically possible for women to spread the virus to women partners through oral sex, although AIDS educators and physicians express a gamut of opinions about the actual likelihood of this happening. Some say the risks are few, and others advise caution.

If you're not absolutely sure whether or not your woman partner is infected with the AIDS virus, we think it's safer if you use a dental dam during oral sex. We think it's imperative for you to use one if your partner's menstruating, because blood is a major vehicle for carrying the AIDS virus (see the section on eroticizing latex for some ideas on how dental dams can be playfully incorporated).

Whether your partner is a woman or a man, in order for sex to be safe, you have to communicate what you want, and you have to take responsibility for your own health and happiness. The first step is to decide that you will have sex only if it's going to be as safe as possible for both of you. Once you've made this agreement with yourself, then you need to be sure that your partner also agrees. This is where communication is so important.

If you feel that you are being responsible for the health of both your partner and yourself, and your partner is showing no responsibility, it may be best to consider getting out of the relationship.

# *Eroticizing Latex*

Although latex doesn't feel like naked skin, or smell or taste like it, it can create special sensations of its own, and as you explore these, you can learn to enjoy them. It all starts in the mind. As you incorporate latex into your fantasies and masturbatory patterns, as well as into your experiences with a partner, then condoms, dams, and gloves can become sex enhancers rather than awkward devices for sexual hygiene.

Our reporters affirm that if you begin by associating great sex with safer sex, then the actual thought of choosing the right condom or glove and putting it on can become a turn-on. And if using condoms, dams, or gloves is playful and involves both partners, you can maintain sexual momentum without interrupting the mood.

## Eroticizing Condoms

Patricia, the partner surrogate you met in Chapter 2, stresses that if you put condoms on as soon as the action begins, then you can be free to be more spontaneous as things heat up. You don't have to wait until your partner has a full erection. In fact, to avoid contact with pre-ejaculatory fluid, it's safer not to wait. Also, it can be much more playful to start with a soft penis, says Patricia. You can stimulate him while you're rolling the condom on.

Patricia offers four steps for the complex sport of clothing a flaccid penis in rubber. As we read them over, they sound a bit like putting a child's erector set together in the wee hours of Christmas morning. But once you get the hang of it, it's really quite simple, and a lot of fun for both of you. Here's how:

1. Place a dab of spermicide in the tip, if the condom is not already lubricated with spermicide. Then, with both hands, stretch the condom and place it over the tip of the penis.

2. Hold the condom and the tip of the penis with one hand and gently stretch the penis up and out.

3. Use your other hand to roll the condom all the way to the base of the penis, being sure you don't get snarled up in his pubic hair.

4. Play with him as you roll the condom on by continuing to hold the tip of the penis with one hand and stroke the shaft and the condom downward with the other. As he becomes erect, be sure the condom still fits snugly all the way to the base of his penis.

Practice makes perfect. You can rehearse the art of putting a condom on, even without the presence of a partner.

Take one out of the packet, feel it, sniff it, lick it, and then unroll it onto your fingers.

You don't have to stop with your fingers; you can put it on a banana, a cucumber, a broom handle, or even your big toe. If you want to rehearse for a flaccid penis, eat the banana first, and practice on the skin.

Practice not trapping air in the tip.

When we asked Patricia what was the most sensual and provocative thing she could think of to do with a condom, she replied: "Going down on him and sliding the condom on with my mouth."

Another surrogate informed us: "I do it for fun, and I'll be very obvious about it. The guy loves it, of course, and being able to do it gives me a feeling of great control. When you get good, you can sneak it on him without him even knowing it. If I'm with a guy who thinks condoms are a real drag—you know, the kind who say: 'I never use them, they're not natural and they interrupt spontaneity'—I don't stop sex to argue with him. I just start fooling around, and I'll have one on him before he knows what's hit him."

It's not as easy as it sounds.

We practiced on cucumbers while Patricia talked us down over the phone, relaying instructions like an air-traffic controller in a B movie. On the first run, the condoms were headed the wrong way and we sucked them into our mouths instead of neatly sheathing the cucumber with them. On the next run, they sprang out and bounced onto the floor.

But with perseverance and a sense of humor, we think anyone can get it. Here are directions from the control tower.

## *Patricia's Oral Condom Roll*

Use an unlubricated condom. Unroll it a little to loosen it up, and then roll it back.

With your mouth nearly shut, place the condom in front of your teeth with your upper and lower lips over the condom. Be sure it's facing so it will unroll the right way (this is where we almost inhaled it).

Hold the penis (or practice cucumber) firmly in the palm of your hand, and grasp the rim of the condom with the thumb and index finger of the same hand. Tighten your lips and push the rim down over the penis (or cucumber), using your lips and your tongue to guide it in a firm but suggestive motion.

When it comes to the real thing, the more playful, exciting and teasing you are, the more aroused your partner and you will be.

Don't use the same condom in intercourse that you've used on a cucumber. Use a new one with each sexual interaction and each sexual situation.

### *...and a Few of Patricia's Other Sensual Tricks*

Talk. Talk about which condoms turn you on. Talk about what you plan to do to him. Talk about what you wish he'd do to you.

Excite him by gently rubbing the top of a condom around the tip of his penis before rolling it on. A dab (and just a dab) of lubricant inside the reservoir tip can also heighten his pleasure.

Try playing with condoms together in nonsexual situations, like while you're watching television. Put them on each other's hands and feet and noses. Remember those clowns at children's parties that made little doggies out of balloons? You can blow up condoms and make penises and breasts out of them.

Try a spectrum of colors—white, black, red, green. And conduct a comparison test on textures. Ultrathin feels different from thicker latex.

If you really don't like the taste, you don't have to just grin and bear it. Try these tricks to mask and take away the residual taste:

> Sip citrus juice or suck a mint or sour candy before, during, and after putting latex in your mouth.
>
> Slather his condom with something you *do* like the taste of; honey and syrup are safe choices, because they won't deteriorate the latex.

Remember that some people are allergic to scented condoms and dental dams. If you or your partner experience irritation, redness, or itching, try another brand.

## Dental Dams

We asked Dell Williams, who owns the women's pleasure boutique Eve's Garden, to tell us about a new concept in latex lingerie—one that would free hands during oral sex, and provide some playfulness for partners. At this writing, she's having her seamstress sew up some erotic gear to hold replaceable latex dams. She calls it the Eve's Garden Chastity Belt, and wearing one, you can express yourself in lace, leather, or bright red satin.

If you're good with a needle, you can handcraft some fetching disposable latex undies yourself, or make an inscrutable, mouth-covering mask to don during oral sex. We wonder when the women's magazines will begin showing them as fashion items and providing patterns so you can whip some up for your holiday gift list.

## Gloves and Your G Spot

Your partner can use latex gloves, along with a water-soluble lubricant, to tease and stimulate your G spot.

Are there other areas in the vagina that feel sensitive to you or your partner? Experiment, and remember that stimulating different areas of the vagina and experiencing new sensations may take a little getting used to for both of you.

## A Note about the G Spot

The G spot, or Grafenberg spot, is a sensitive area located inside the vagina in the front wall, about halfway between the back of the pubic bone and the cervix, the part of the uterus that protrudes into the back of the vagina and feels like the tip of your nose.

This area swells when it's stimulated, and in some women, stimulation results in an orgasmic response that feels different from the orgasms you get from clitoral stimulation. Some women report that the orgasm from G-spot stimulation feels more like the orgasm from intercourse. Some women report that they ejaculate a fluid from their urethra when the G spot is stimulated (other women report they ejaculate from stimulation of the clitoris).

Your partner's fingers can stimulate this delightful part of your anatomy. For your safety and your partner's, those fingers should be wearing latex gloves that have been lubricated with a water-soluble substance containing at least 5 percent N-9.

Ask your partner to use a "come here" motion with one or two latex-clad fingers as they stimulate the front wall of the vagina, and join in an experiment to find out everything you both always wanted to know about your G spot.

- Exactly where is your G spot located?
- Does it swell when it's stimulated?
- How does it feel to you and your partner through latex?
- Is this fun for your partner as well as for you? If not, don't continue the stimulation.
- What does the stimulation feel like to you?
- Do you have an urge to urinate?
- Do you have an absolutely irresistible urge to come to orgasm?

You might enjoy stimulation of both G spot and clitoris at the same time. You and your partner can experiment until you find out what genital areas are most pleasurable. And you can treat yourselves to the added pleasure of talking about it together as well as doing it.

When it comes to giving pleasure, latex gloves can also be worn to stimulate your partner's prostate gland. This is the male equivalent of the G spot, a sensitive area in the front wall of the man's rectum. Some men enjoy having the penis stimulated at the same time the prostate is being stimulated. For safety's sake, use a latex condom on the penis and a latex glove on your hand—and your favorite safe lubricant on both.

This information about the G spot and women's ejaculation was first popularized in 1982 in *The G Spot and Other Recent Discoveries about Human Sexuality*. The information was offered to affirm women's experiences and help women who had this type of response to feel better about themselves; it was not offered to set a new sexual goal. We feel the same way about the information in this book. Do incorporate the latex factor into your sexual and sensual interactions as it feels right and good to you. But please don't interpret the information in this chapter as a goal that you're supposed to achieve.

## A Note about Anal Stimulation

The walls of the rectum are very fragile and easy to injure. This makes any kind of anal stimulation a prime way to spread the AIDS virus. This refers not only to anal intercourse practiced by gay men (which is the main reason AIDS has spread so rapidly through this community), but to heterosexual anal intercourse and to stimulation of the anus with fingers, whether your partner is a man or a woman.

Some sexologists report that the staggeringly high incidence of AIDS among women in Central Africa may be partly due to the widespread practice of anal intercourse there—a consequence of the widespread ritual of infibulation (sewing shut or otherwise closing the vaginal openings of little girls and young women).

Because of the extreme risk of transmission of the AIDS virus, we cannot recommend anal stimulation as an even moderately safe choice of sexual activity. However, if you choose it, and are not 100 percent sure of your partner, *be scrupulously careful about using the protection of latex gloves, and be sure you use lots of water-soluble lubrication.* (Remember that N-9 hasn't yet been proved safe for anal use.)

A word from our faithful Frogwoman before she glides off into the sunset: By inundating you with this material, we're not trying to equate sex with rubber. We feel that learning how to use latex is only one part of taking charge of your sexual safety. We urge you to use the information in this chapter in the spirit in which it is offered—that is, in context with the rest of your sexual and emotional relationship.

The distressing truth is that there is as yet no cure or effective vaccine for AIDS or herpes. Even though latex barriers are not completely reliable, they may save much misery by helping prevent the transmission of herpes, and they may save millions of lives by helping prevent transmission of AIDS.

But handing out condoms in college dorms and at safe-sex rallies is not enough. To make sex truly safe, we need a change in our national attitude. We need to stop thinking about "sex" as goal-oriented intercourse, and we need to stop thinking about women as objects of that kind of sex.

We can't change the whole nation. We can only change ourselves. Every woman who learns to truly value herself and clearly express her own ideas about what sexuality means to her brings all of us closer to being able to understand sexual intimacy as *relationships*—relationships in which emotions are as important as physical thrills and in which physical thrills include many, many events other than intercourse.

With this understanding, you don't have to think of taking care of your sexual safety as a deprivation. Even the latex factor can be an opportunity for personal expansion and pleasurable adventure.

# SAFER-SEX ROAD MAP FOR CHAPTER 4: YOUR LATEX EXPERIENCES

In Chapter 4 you've read a lot of information about using latex and spermicides to make sex safer. This Safer-Sex Road Map is to help you discover more about how *you* feel about the latex factor, and how *you* respond to making love through latex. It is designed to help you see graphically the specific ways you can minimize risks and maximize pleasure during your sexual encounters.

## *Latex Shopping List*

Make a list of all of the safer-sex paraphernalia you have purchased or plan to purchase. Include the brand name, best store to purchase from, price, and your feelings about using them.

Condoms

________________________________________

________________________________________

________________________________________

Dental Dams

________________________________________

________________________________________

________________________________________

Latex Gloves

________________________________________

________________________________________

________________________________________

Lubricants

________________________________________

________________________________________

________________________________________

Other

________________________________________

________________________________________

________________________________________

# *Safer-Sex Thrills Chart*

To help you assess your personal reactions, rate your experiences with the following safer-sex devices. Use a 1-to-10 scale (10 for ecstasy):

| | *Sensation* | *Taste* | *Smell* | *Peace of Mind* | *Partner Satisfaction* | *Overall Satisfaction* |
|---|---|---|---|---|---|---|
| **Condoms:** | | | | | | |
| Lubricated | | | | | | |
| Unlubricated | | | | | | |
| Colored | | | | | | |
| Ribbed | | | | | | |
| With Safety Seal | | | | | | |
| **Dental Dams:** | | | | | | |
| Colored | | | | | | |
| Flavored | | | | | | |
| **Latex Gloves:** | | | | | | |
| Unpowdered | | | | | | |
| Powdered | | | | | | |
| Scented | | | | | | |
| **Lubricants:** | | | | | | |
| Jelly | | | | | | |
| Cream | | | | | | |
| Foam | | | | | | |
| **Other** | | | | | | |

## *Personal Safer-Sex Commitment*

To make my sex life safer, I commit myself to doing the following about using and communicating about condoms, gloves, dental dams, and spermicides containing N-9.

______________________________________________

______________________________________________

______________________________________________

______________________________________________

# CHAPTER 5

## *What about Flying Solo?*

"My life would be so much easier if I didn't end up in lousy relationships just because I get desperate for the sex," Deborah complains. "But I have about a million hang-ups about touching myself. How can I get over them?"

In this age of AIDS and other STDs, Deborah's complaint is a vital one, especially for women who do not have long-term, trustworthy, monogamous partners. The very safest technique of all for genital satisfaction is self-stimulation. *You cannot transmit any sexually transmitted disease to yourself, and that includes the AIDS virus.*

A major step to overcoming hang-ups like Deborah's is education. Although accurate information may not be enough to dispel all of your fears and confusion about self-stimulation, at least it may help you pinpoint where it is you're feeling blocked.

Let's begin this education process by saying that not only is solo sex safe, but it's also good for you. Many doctors and therapists acknowledge that masturbation can improve both your physical health and your mental outlook.[1] Researchers point out that some women report more physical satisfaction from it than from partner sex, particularly from intercourse.[2]

Although studies show that 80 percent of today's women do indeed masturbate,[3] they also show that the result of masturbation is not always pleasure, release, and relaxation. In fact, it's more likely to be guilt and shame. Despite the potential benefits of masturbation, millions of women in our culture today feel like Deborah. They're beset by self-recriminations after they've touched themselves for sexual pleasure.

And some women are too scared to touch themselves at all. Even thinking about it may bring on waves of disgust or horror, or may trigger vehement arguments against it. Some have trouble articulating exactly where these feelings come from. Others can point exactly to some traumatic event in childhood (like being discovered *in flagrante*), or they can remember lectures and moralizing, or the blanket disapproval of a parent or some other authority figure.

How, in the course of history, has something as enjoyable and empowering as sexual self-pleasure become so fraught with guilt, fear, and disgust?

Nobody can say exactly why masturbation taboos and scare tactics began, but sexologists concur that an age-old way to control any population is to instill fear of sexual feelings and sexual behaviors. This is a tactic that's enjoying a comeback in our society today, as some of our religious leaders and politicians preach that AIDS is sent by an angry God to punish people for being gay or being promiscuous.

Our personal theory is that masturbation taboos originally had to do with taming women—leading them to loathe their own bodies and fear their sexual energy so they'd stay at home with their mates and bring up the babies instead of gallivanting about in the bush looking for adventures. Over the centuries, of course, taboos against self-pleasure applied to men, too.

When did the taboos begin? Again, no one knows exactly.

The ancient Romans ensured that the word "masturbation" would have negative connotations by giving it a blackly negative definition: "to defile with the hand," from two Latin words—*manus* (hand) and *stuprare* (to defile).

By the time the Judeo-Christian fathers got around to writing down the doctrines that were the basis of much of our social and legal systems, self-pleasure was already an "unnatural" act, "against the law of God." To fundamentalist western religions, masturbation has traditionally been a sin. Jews, Catholics, and Protestants have been exposed to centuries of teaching about the immorality of masturbation. As recently as 1975, a Vatican pronouncement, the "Declaration on Certain

Questions Concerning Sexual Ethics," stated that masturbation is "an intrinsically and seriously disordered act."[4]

By the eighteenth century the medical profession took up religion's anti-masturbation banner: the Age of Enlightenment might well be called the Age of Masturbatory Insanity.

In 1760, a Swiss physician named Tissot wrote his seminal work: *Onania, or a Treatise upon the Disorders Produced by Masturbation*. This gave "scientific" support to the negative view of self-stimulation. It established as indisputable fact that disturbances like insanity, poor eyesight, indigestion, and impotence were the consequences of masturbation or "onanism" (mistakenly named for Onan, the biblical character who "spilled his seed on the ground" rather than marry his brother's widow). In the United States, Dr. Benjamin Rush, the father of American psychiatry, added that "self-pollution" produced pulmonary consumption, vertigo, epilepsy, and loss of memory.[5] It was claimed that further symptoms were hollow cheeks, marks on the face, irritability, baldness, and dysmenorrhea.

Treatments for the disorder included chastity belts, mittens spiked with iron thorns, suturing the vaginal opening, and surgical removal of the clitoris. Newly publicized letters show that Sigmund Freud actually prescribed nasal surgery as a cure for hysteria, a disorder he diagnosed as being caused by his patient's habit of masturbating.[6]

Don't laugh. Some of these bizarre beliefs were held into this century, and what's more, some are held even today. As recently as 1961, a survey of five U.S. medical schools indicated that half the students and a fifth of the faculty believed that masturbation could lead to mental illness.[7]

## *Down-There Myth-Information*

As we approach the twenty-first century, some of the ancient myths about masturbation continue to influence us. If our earliest message about sex is: "Don't ever touch yourself Down There!" this has a tremendous impact on our self-image and on our sexual behavior as we grow older. When this message is repeatedly reinforced not only by authority figures when we're growing up, but by peer pressure as well, women like Deborah feel they have no other choice than to acquiesce. And they also hasten to protect their children from scorn and punishment by training them at an early age that "down there" is off limits.

Let's look at some of the myths Deborah said she grew up with. She still believes some of these, which makes it difficult for her to overcome her hang-ups about self-pleasuring.

Check each of the following myths you've heard at some time in your life. Where did you hear each one? Which ones did you believe? Which ones do you still believe? Use the blank space at the end to add other myths that may have influenced you. Jot down your present response to those myths in the "Facts" column.

| *Myths* | *Facts* |
|---|---|
| Masturbation causes:<br>Blindness<br>Hair on the palms<br>Pimples<br>Insanity<br><br>Masturbation is a sign of:<br>Emotional illness<br>Immaturity<br>Weak-mindedness<br>Inability to relate to a partner | These are all golden oldies, originally designed to inhibit your sexual freedom.<br>Our favorite response to these kinds of scare tactics comes from the little girl who said to her uncle when he warned her she'd go blind: "Couldn't I just do it 'til I need to wear glasses?" |
| Masturbation can be addicting: Once you start you'll never stop. | Indeed, it may feel so good that sometimes you don't want to stop. But desire does not equal addiction.<br>Does masturbating generate more problems than pleasure? |

(*continued*)

| *Myths* | *Facts* |
|---|---|
| | Does it control your life? If you can answer No, you're not a self-pleasure junkie.<br>If you're getting pressure from your partner about how much you're masturbating, then that's a problem of relationship, not of self-stimulation. |
| God can spot a masturbator—and so can your minister, your school principal, and your Aunt Myrna. | There are no signs and symptoms of masturbation, despite what Freud and others have said. So no matter who claims to be able to tell, they can't.<br>A woman we interviewed tells us she longs for someone to accuse her so she can reply: "You're absolutely right. Of course I masturbate. And if I keep on doing it I'll be happier and healthier and live longer, too." |
| And a few myths that are specific to women: | |
| Women don't masturbate. That's just for teenagers and gay men. | Almost everybody, all over the world, does it at one time or another in their lives. And that includes most women. |
| If you masturbate, you can't relate sexually to a partner; you'll never enjoy intercourse. | Sex therapists often prescribe masturbation as step one in learning to relate sexually to a partner. Quitting is not likely to help a woman enjoy intercourse. What may help is to improve the quality of intercourse, and to choose other sexual activities you do like, such as kissing, fondling, or massaging. |

| *Myths* | *Facts* |
|---|---|
| If you masturbate, you won't be able to get pregnant. | Masturbation does not affect conception. |
| If you masturbate, your genital lips will grow (like Pinocchio's nose?), a telltale sign to your doctor. | Your genitals are unique and distinct, just like your facial features. Women's genital lips come in many delightful sizes, shapes, and shades of color. The size is determined genetically, just like the size of your clitoris or any other part of your genitals. |
| Your influential myths: | Your responses to your myths: |
| ______________________ | ______________________ |
| ______________________ | ______________________ |
| ______________________ | ______________________ |

# *Why Fly Solo?*

One of the respondents in *The Hite Report* remarked about her experiences of self-pleasure: "At least I know I'm going to bed with someone I like."[8] But we've heard many women sigh: "The problem is, I *don't* like myself."

So the issue of self-pleasure brings up not only the myths, taboos and injunctions that are specific to touching yourself "down there," but also some larger issues of self-care and self-worth, those issues that are specific to all aspects of being a woman.

We believe that pleasurable masturbating means more than self-indulgence (though we don't think there's anything at all the matter with a bit of *that* on a rainy Saturday afternoon). We believe it means helping you develop a healthy relationship with yourself.

Further, we believe that women who can't pleasure themselves are missing out on a valuable safe-sex technique, and this is one that really *is* safe, for it eliminates the risk factor that's built in to sex with any partner who's not free of the AIDS virus or any other STDs. Moreover, women who can't pleasure themselves are likely to perpetuate negative attitudes in their children, and there will be yet another generation deprived of knowledge that may literally save their lives.

Self-pleasuring can fulfill at least four functions in your life now.

First of all, it feels good. You can give yourself pleasure whenever you want—after a hard day, in the middle of a boring task, or just for fun. And your capacity for self-pleasure is with you your whole life long, as a child and an adult.

Second, you don't need a partner to do it. Self-pleasuring can provide sexual release when you don't have a partner, or when one is not available. It can keep you from Deborah's fate of leaping into a relationship with someone else just to have sex, no matter how inappropriate the relationship might be. By the way, you don't always have to masturbate alone. Later in this chapter we'll talk about how to share it.

Third, it can provide self-knowledge. If you can allow yourself to experience good feelings, it can help you learn to like yourself better by helping you know what feels good to you. This is information you can communicate to your partner, if you choose.[9]

Fourth, and most relevant to our subject, self-pleasuring is an absolutely safe way to explore your sexuality—safe for you, safe for your partner.

> **REMEMBER** To feel sexually fulfilled, you don't need to have sexual intercourse with another person.

## *How Do Women Do It?*

How do women fly solo? There's no right or wrong way. No "normal" or "abnormal." Each woman is unique and has her own pattern. In fact, in their study of human sexual response, Masters and Johnson found that none of their female research volunteers masturbated in exactly the same way.[10]

Let's start with the relationship aspect of masturbation. First and foremost, masturbation is a sexual relationship with the most important partner you'll ever have—you.

To learn to enjoy stimulating yourself (or to intensify enjoyment if you're already an old hand), do yourself the honor of observing some of the same safe-sex routines you would with any other partner. Don't just start being physical without checking out your own feelings first and setting the scene so you're private and comfortable.

Above all, communicate with yourself about what feels good, what feels appropriate, and what feels safe. If you don't already do these automatically, or if you're confused about how to practice them, refer to some of the relationship-building exercises in Chapters 1 and 2.

In terms of physical satisfaction, you'll have to experiment and find out which positions, movements, and stimulations feel best to you. You may want to vary your methods from time to time.

Although many women report extremely powerful orgasms through masturbation, we want to emphasize that overall pleasure and self-caring are just as important as the final fireworks. If your only goal is orgasm, you may miss many of the wonderful feelings along the way.

> **HOT TIP** Allow an orgasm to happen if it happens, but focus on *all* the sensations and feelings your self-stimulation provides.

## Fingers

Some women like to touch themselves by slowly caressing their whole body, while others go directly for the genitals. Some women lie on their stomachs, others on their backs or sides. Some use their right hand, some use their left, others use both.

Many women prefer rhythmically stroking or pressing the

vulva: Some like to stimulate their whole mons area, others like to pull on their inner lips or excite the clitoral shaft. Some use slow circular motion all the way around; others rub up and down one side or the other. However, very few women report that they like direct stimulation of the tip or glans of the clitoris; it's very sensitive, and direct stimulation can be irritating or downright painful.

There are women who like to stimulate their vaginas by moving their fingers in and out. Some women with long fingers like to reach inside to the front inside vaginal wall and stimulate the exquisitely sensitive G spot with a "come here" motion, but most women cannot reach their G spots with their own fingers. Some like to combine vaginal stimulation with clitoral stimulation.

Some women use a rapid motion, some change their rhythm

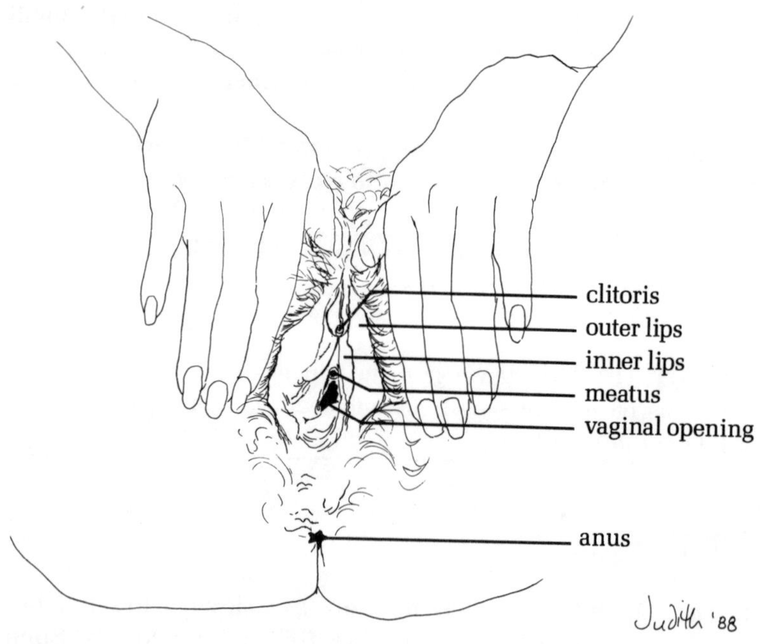


*The external female genitalia*

depending on their degree of sexual arousal. Movements usually become more intense until orgasm. Many women who have talked with us say they continue stimulation all the way through to the end of their orgasm, in contrast to men's typical masturbatory pattern of stopping stimulation at the point of orgasm. Not all women continue stimulating themselves throughout their orgasm, however. Again, what's typical of women's sexuality is its infinite variety of experience. There's no one right way to stimulate yourself.

## Vibrators

Electric vibrators provide a pleasing alternative for some women. One fan pointed out that the only problem she had with vibrators was figuring out what to do for sexual pleasure in a power outage. The electricity can also be a problem if you're traveling to countries with a different voltage system. We have a friend who claims to have blown out all the lights in her hotel in Rome during a moment of ecstasy, so we suggest you bring your electrical converter with your vibrator when you travel to foreign countries.

Vibrators also come in battery-operated models, which some women prefer because they're quieter and gentler and because they don't require an electrical outlet. There are a variety of shapes—from dildos, to little eggs, to doggies with wagging tongues and tails—and your choice will depend on your individual taste and sense of humor.

They're great for travel, too, though we had one friend who was nearly arrested as a potential highjacker when her battery-operated ben-wa balls flicked on inside her suitcase and began ticking like time bombs as she was checking in at the airline counter.

Vibrators are not as versatile and sensitive as fingers, of course, but women can use them in almost as many ways—to stimulate clitoris, vagina, anus, breasts, thighs, and any other place they want to reach. They may use them in combination with their fingers, and sometimes in combination with other sex toys, such as plastic dildos or natural dildos, like vegetables.

What vibrators do best is vibrate. That is, they provide continual, some say inexorable, stimulation without your having to do anything except enjoy.

This makes them ideal for women who want a quick fix, and also for women who are gluttons for prolonged pleasure. As one woman says: "A vibrator saves all that wear and tear on my right hand. I used to get a terrible case of writer's cramp."

Vibrators are also a blessing for women who have problems coming to orgasm, because the continual vibration tends to break through resistances.

And vibrators can be a blessing for women like Deborah, who are still too bound up in old injunctions against masturbation to be able to touch themselves happily with their fingers.

How can you buy a vibrator? You may find a selection in your local drugstore or department store, probably billed as "relaxers" or "face and body massagers" (so if you're shy about shopping, you don't have to describe in lurid detail everything you want it to do for you). You can also order them from shops like Eve's Garden or Good Vibrations that specialize in pleasure accessories for women and make no bones about their erotic purpose (see Chapter 9 for mail-order addresses).

## Thigh Pressure

Another method some women enjoy is squeezing and contracting their thigh muscles while thrusting their genitals against a bed or pillow. Others like to press their thigh muscles together with their legs crossed. Some women can masturbate and reach orgasm by riding a bicycle.[11]

## Water Play

We're all brought up in a culture that values cleanliness next to godliness. But bathing can go way beyond getting clean. Showering or soaking in a tub or Jacuzzi can be a sensual pleasure—solo, or with a partner.

One woman tells us she prefers bathing solo to almost any other kind of sexual encounter. "Sometimes I think maybe my primary relationship is with my plumbing. I have a big old claw-foot tub—the kind you can really stretch out in. It sits away from the wall and has a wonderful brass faucet. If I lie on my back and drape my legs over the sides of the tub I can run water directly onto my clitoris."

Some women have favorite hand-held shower heads. They can adjust the pressure and direct the water exactly where they want it, taking the hit-or-miss out of taking a shower. The fancier ones come with pulsating heads, which some women swear by.

The jets and bubbles in hot tubs or spas are the icing on the cake for some women, not only for genital stimulation, but also for the general relaxation they can bring to body, mind and soul.

We know a woman who's created a lush environment around her hot tub, including tropical plants, continuous-play music, and her own special rubber ducky that bobs on the body-temperature waves: "Some people think the rubber ducky's a joke, but it's a really important part of my sensuality. It reminds me that I can giggle and play like a 5-year-old. What good is it to stand around in front of the jets and come if it isn't any fun? Playing is where the sexuality is, for me."

By the way, you don't have to be one of the rich and famous to own a spa these days. Some are reasonably priced and even portable, so that if you should move, you can take it with you.

## Fantasy

Fantasy is a solo technique you can enjoy any time and any place. Sexual fantasies don't have to happen just during masturbation or physical interactions with a partner; you can have steamy adventures while driving a car, taking a shower, or simply resting with your eyes closed.

You can replay past experiences or change them, look forward to future events or rehearse them. You can enjoy situations that may be too outrageous for you in reality. You can create a sexual life that's exactly the way you desire—and that's absolutely safe.

In fact, some women are able to experience intense sexual pleasure without any physical touching at all. In a study of easily orgasmic women, almost two-thirds of the women reported being able to come to orgasm spontaneously, on fantasy alone, with no other stimulation.[12] This is not a goal we're suggesting you have to strive for, by the way, but many women find they can and do enjoy spontaneous orgasm once they're given a precedent for it, and permission. And it offers you another alternative for safe sex in the age of AIDS.

Researchers say that most women do their fantasizing while masturbating and that most women's fantasies are about their partners. The next most popular subjects for fantasies are activities these women say they'd never do in real life, like pick-up sex with strangers, group sex, forced sex, or sex with another woman.[13] Favorite fantasies women have shared with us include making love in an elevator (pushing the emergency stop button just long enough to come) and making love with film stars from Robert Redford to Ingrid Bergman.

Some women prefer reruns: "I like to remember my lover bathing me, feeding me, and then making slow, sensual love to me."

Other women prefer future fantasies: "I'm tied to a bed, unable to move, while my lover licks and sucks all over my body. He tells me exactly what he's going to do, and then he does it. I am totally unable to stimulate him in any way, or control any of his actions. I love it when he enters me, and I beg him for more.

"What's so exciting about this is that it's very hard for me to let go in real life, and this fantasy allows me to be out of control. I'm a bit embarrassed about the domination part. Maybe I'll get to the point where I can fantasize about controlling him—or better still, about us both having equal control."

Fantasy is not the same as reality, and thinking about something does not necessarily mean that you want to do it or that you will act it out. And not all sexual fantasies are pleasurable. You can fantasize about rape, or being rejected by your lover, or even about contracting AIDS. You can then use your fantasies to rehearse how to deal with these events or prevent them from occurring.

**HOT TIP** No one will ever get AIDS from a fantasy, even if the behaviors in the fantasy are unsafe.

Some therapists and women's groups suggest erotic literature, especially for women who are just learning to masturbate and fantasize. There are books replete with women's fantasies written by women for women, such as Nancy Friday's *My Secret Garden*, and Lonnie Barbach's *Erotic Interludes*. Reading can help when you don't like your current fantasies, or when you simply want some new ideas.

However you decide to use fantasy, though, we wish you a most creative bon voyage. We hope that you'll learn and grow from all your fantasies and that your lusciously enjoyable ones will bring you waves of sexual arousal.

## *Learning How*

Earlier in this chapter we pointed out that having accurate information is an essential step for overcoming hang-ups about masturbation. Another equally important step is practice.

But suppose you've never masturbated. Or suppose, like Deborah, you have fears about it, or feel guilty or ashamed. Or maybe you've tried and nothing much happens. You don't have to give up on this valuable and entirely safe form of sexual pleasure. And don't think you're too old to learn. We've talked with women in their seventies who've just begun.

Here are five more things to try:

1. **Read:** You might start with two positive and instructive books on the subject: Lonnie Barbach's *For Yourself*, and Betty Dodson's *Sex for One*.

2. **Join a women's support group:** If you can find a group that deals with sexuality, this may be an ideal atmosphere in which to dispel old myths and learn some new ways of relating to yourself sexually. Other women sharing similar concerns can help you know you're not alone. And their openness can help you understand that touching yourself for pleasure can feel good, and not evil or sick. Sex therapist Barbach designed the first "preorgasmic" groups for women, and *For Yourself* is the book that describes them.

3. **Discover more about your own sexual history:** This can help you understand which of your attitudes are outdated and which ones you want to keep (see guidelines for taking a Self-Pleasure History in the Safe-Sex Road Map section at the end of this chapter).

   Keep a journal of your feelings and attitudes so you can see which ones change over time.

4. **Make a time commitment with yourself:** Set aside a few minutes every day or evening as "feel-good time" just for you, and lock the door if you have to. Start with ten-minute stints, and work your way up to forty-five minutes at a time.

   Do some deep breathing, play some relaxing music, fantasize, read some of the erotica mentioned above.

Get to know yourself better:

- Look at yourself naked in a full-length mirror. Focus on what you like best about yourself.
- Lie on your back or sit, and hold a hand mirror so that you can see your vulva. Notice how your features are as distinct as your facial features.
- Explore with your hands every inch of your body you can reach, including your vulva.
- Test-drive some vibrators until you determine your favorite.

5. **Teach yourself Kegel exercises:** This is a secret weapon that can not only intensify your orgasms, but also give you pleasure at any time, in any situation, in utter safety, and without anyone knowing. What's more, you can Kegel without even touching yourself. And if you haven't ever had an orgasm and are eager to discover the route to your first one, learning to Kegel may be a key.

Kegels are exercises named for Dr. Arnold Kegel, who developed them in the 1950s to help strengthen the pubococcygeus muscle, or PC for short. This muscle surrounds the vagina and urethra, and it contracts rhythmically during orgasm, so that if you flex and relax it, it can feel very good—like a mini-orgasm, in fact.

Here's a brief lesson in Kegeling. For more complete instructions, and more history, see Chapter 4 of *The G Spot.*[14]

To locate your PC, squat with your legs spread apart, and contract, as if to stop a flow of urine. You can feel your muscle tighten across your whole genital area.

To feel your PC in action, lie down and put a finger into your vagina and contract your PC until you squeeze your finger. You can also open two fingers inside your vagina and feel your PC muscle close them together like a pair of scissors. If you can't squeeze your fingers with your vagina, then your PC could use some toning.

To begin: Squeeze your PC muscle for three seconds and then relax for three seconds. Do this ten times, three times a day.

Gradually increase to ten seconds of squeezing and ten seconds of relaxing. And remember, we're talking about pleasure here, not training for the Olympics. *The relaxing is just as important as the contracting.*

And don't forget to breathe!

Holding your breath usually keeps you from feeling pleasure (or any other feeling). Allowing yourself to breathe, deeply and naturally, is tantamount to saying Yes to emotion. An effective way to synchronize pleasure breathing with Kegels is to inhale each time you contract and exhale as you relax. To extend pleasurable feelings you might want to combine Kegels with the Pleasure Mantra described in Chapter 1.

As you get proficient, vary the exercise with flicks, in which you contract and relax very quickly. Do a series of quick flicks three times a day along with the longer exercise. This will help you gain more control over your muscle.

Increase the number in each series until you're doing as many as 50 at a time—150 a day. You don't have to alter your routine to fit in your Kegels. Women tell us they Kegel when they stop at red lights or answer the phone. One woman tells us she does Kegel exercises during meetings to keep alert.

Many women report that they feel turned on as they do the Kegel exercises. This is perfectly normal. Enjoy the feeling!

## *Sharing with a Partner*

Solo sex doesn't always have to take place alone, behind closed doors. Sharing your self-knowledge and methods with a partner can be intimate and arousing for both of you.

Sharing fantasies or showing how your body responds can open up channels of communication that can enhance your sex and deepen your relationship. Demonstrating your solo preferences not only helps your partner understand how to stimulate you most effectively, it can also convey a profound sense of trust. It tells your partner that you're willing to risk your most private experiences.

Your partner's response can be an enormous indication to you of love, respect, and caring. This, in turn, can increase your self-confidence and excitement—feelings your partner is sure to notice and very possibly reflect back to you with renewed energy. Communication is a two-way street, and sharing like this can quickly escalate the feelings between you.

And this is a kind of sexual sharing that's completely safe. You can't get AIDS, or give it, from telling your fantasies, or from showing a partner where you like to be stimulated, what type of pressure you like, what rhythm feels best, how you like to have an orgasm, and what happens to your body as you experience all this. And of course you can always play tit-for-tat by asking your partner to share fantasies and masturbatory patterns with you.

But this kind of show-and-tell may be easier for us to talk about here than it is for you to carry out in actuality. After all, as women, we're trained to take care of our partners, not ourselves, and that can hold true whether your partner's a man or a woman.

And we've been taught that good girls don't have fun, or at least not *much* fun. As one woman said: "God forbid I should be taking time for me when I could be doing something useful, like massaging my partner."

We've also been taught to believe our partners are responsible for giving us an orgasm. Particularly if your partner's a man, chances are that both you and he have been socialized to believe that he should be in charge. In addition, you may both have been socialized to believe that he owns your orgasm, or at least has first rights to it, making sure he gives it to you his way, not yours.

Pleasuring yourself in the presence of a partner, or opening up to talk about your sexual fantasies, may mean going against all your good-girl upbringing, and may go against your partner's upbringing, too. Even if you update your own belief system, you may have a hard time convincing him that self-pleasuring is OK for you and that show-and-tell is OK for him to witness. These actions may be physically safe because they don't expose either of you to STDs, including the AIDS virus, but they may feel like the riskiest things you can do emotionally.

There's the added risk that you might be fantasizing about someone else, or about activities your partner can't do, and that sharing this could be painful or hurtful to your partner. We can't tell you how to assess whether it might be more pleasurable (or at least more growthful) to share, or whether it's the better part of valor to keep your sexual fantasies to yourself. Only you can know that, and each instance is individual.

We can point out, however, that because women have been socialized to be extrasensitively tuned in to their partners' feelings (or at least to what they *imagine* their partners are feeling), we sometimes disable our partners when we think we're protecting them. There's a fine line between being lovingly responsive women and being smotheringly overresponsible women "who love too much."

Overresponsibility can be just as numbing to your partner as it may be exhausting for you. If you want your partner to relate to you in the fullest possible way, you may have to risk whatever the reaction may be when you share your fantasies.

What can you do to make sharing your self-pleasuring experiences with a partner the safest encounter possible?

## Tips for Safe Show-and-Tell

- Remember that safe and safer sex means changing some of your attitudes and actions, even if that may be hard for you and your partner at first. Take it step by step and give yourself permission to take as much time as you need to ease into this new behavior.
- Remember that self-responsibility is the key concept in safe sex. You, and you alone, are responsible for your own sexual thoughts, emotions, and physical responses, whether they're a result of self-pleasuring or a sexual encounter with a partner.
- Remember that you have a right to your thoughts and feelings, whatever they are.
- Remember that no one knows your body and how it responds as well as you do.
- Put yourself in your partner's shoes (even if your partner doesn't happen to be wearing shoes at this moment). How would you feel about witnessing your partner's fantasies or physical self-pleasure?
- Check it out with your partner, especially if you're not sure about the reactions you might get. This may be a chance for the two of you to enter into some valuable discussion about what sexuality means to you and about what sexual safety means.

- Be aware that hearing your fantasies or watching you arouse yourself may be a tremendous turn-on for your partner.

## A Pocket Phrase Guide to Self-Pleasure with a Partner

| *When You Feel...* | *You Can Say...* |
|---|---|
| Embarrassed | I'm really shy about this, but I'd like to show you what I do when I masturbate. And then maybe you'll show me what you do, and then maybe we can do it together. |
| Exposed | I know I said I wanted to do this, but now I feel vulnerable and scared. I wish you'd give me a hug and reassure me that it's still OK. |
| As if you're taking too much time for yourself | I know you reassured me that this was OK with you, but I feel as if we're spending too much time just on me. Will you please promise to tell me the minute you begin getting bored and restless? |
| Wonderful | This feels terrific. I'm really happy you encouraged me! |
| Connected to your partner | You've helped me make this feel so natural. I hope you'll show me what you do. |
| Released | Sigh.... |

# SAFE-SEX ROAD MAP FOR CHAPTER 5: YOUR PERSONAL FLIGHT PLAN

In this chapter you've read about the history of self-pleasuring and about how other women feel. This Safe-Sex Road Map is to help you discover more about how *you* feel and to help you understand specifics of how flying solo might be a valuable safe-sex technique for you at any age or stage in your life.

## *Personal Self-Pleasure History*

Taking a detailed history of your personal experiences is one way to provide yourself with information about self-pleasuring and the role it plays in your life now. Before you begin, be aware that focused history-taking can bring up memories that may have been long forgotten, and raise feelings of all kinds, from the joy of sensuous discovery to infant rage at discovery of adult control.

You can take your own self-pleasure history by writing down answers to the following questions, or you can ask a trusted friend or partner to ask you these questions and listen to your answers. The friend or partner route can add dimension to the experience.

First, it gives you a chance to talk about events that may have been taboo. Some women feel as if a great weight has lifted when they can finally open up and utter the first words. "I thought a chasm was going to open up and swallow me if I talked about it, but all that happened was that I cried because I was so relieved."

Second, a friend or partner can facilitate the history-taking process by asking you to clarify or elaborate where you can't easily answer, or where you have a great many feelings.

A friend or partner can give you support and validation. And you can ask this person to share equally in the adventure by reversing roles when you're through, so that you can help take her or his self-pleasure history.

Feel free to take some liberties with the history that follows. Add questions at will. And if there are questions that seem not to apply to you, substitute questions that do apply.

1. What are some of the messages about masturbation that you received from your family when you were growing up?
2. What are some of the messages you received from teachers, clergy, doctors, or other important people?
3. Did you think masturbation was only for men and boys? If so, what led you to think this?
4. Who did you talk to about masturbation when you were growing up?
5. Do you think anyone ever tried to stop you from masturbating?
6. When did you first masturbate?
7. If you masturbated as a child, did you "forget" how sometime before you were an adult?
8. How did you learn how to masturbate?
9. How do you masturbate now? Do you use fingers, thigh pressure, vibrator, water, or other?
10. How often do you masturbate?
11. How much time do you spend?
12. Describe a favorite experience.
13. Describe an experience masturbating with a partner.
14. Describe three ways you think masturbation could increase the safety of your present sex life.

## *My Safe-Sex Fantasy*

**1.** Write out your own erotic fantasy. Use your favorite old standby if you have one. Otherwise start from scratch—and enjoy!

Make sure to include details that will flesh out the experience: setting, lighting, temperature, scents, props, timing, and duration.

- What's happening in your fantasy?
- Describe the partner or partners (if any).
- How do *you* look, feel, and smell?
- What are your physical and emotional responses?
- What's most satisfying to you about this encounter?

You can write as outrageously as you want. Remember, your English teacher is not going to be having a look at this one.

**2.** Rewrite your fantasy to include techniques for safe sex.

- How do you make sex safe in your new fantasy?
- How do you eroticize making sex safe?

Use all your creativity as you dream of future safe encounters. You can decide later if you want to share this with a flesh-and-blood partner.

## *Personal Safe-Sex Commitment*

In order to gain more self-knowledge, I commit myself to spending time alone learning more about myself and my body in the following way. In addition, I make the following commitment to share my self-pleasuring with my partner:

______________________________________________

______________________________________________

______________________________________________

______________________________________________

# CHAPTER 6

## *Teaching Your Partner to Play*

In the zeal for safety, it's possible to lose sight of pleasure and play, which, after all, are major reasons for having sex. And while it's true that many women have to give up certain ways they used to behave sexually prior to the AIDS epidemic, our message to you is as full of hope in this chapter as it is in earlier ones: Sexual responsibility does not mean you can't have fun. In fact, some of the most satisfying pleasures are ones you don't have to give up.

No matter what sexual activities you choose to engage in, your enjoyment of them depends in large part on how fully you can allow yourself to play. Whether you're searching for ways to start a new relationship without the danger of infection, or whether you're wanting to enhance the sexual excitement with your ongoing partner, your natural sense of play can be a delightful and effective safe-sex technique—valuable to develop along with self-assertion, relationship building, outercourse, latex skills, and flying solo.

And teaching your partner to play can more than double your own inventiveness and satisfaction. In fact, this is your chance to expand the quick-and-easy method of sex with some safe delights, ones you may have been wishing for all along but which may not have been possible as long as the focus of sex was firmly fixed on intercourse, or anchored in a habit of genital stimulation with a goal of orgasm.

But if you're like many of the women who've talked with us, playing may not come easily to you. You may be a victim of the sexual work ethic, that good-girl training which says your job in sex is to please your partner, not to have fun yourself.

So before you can teach your partner to play *your* way, you may need to find out more about what your way is. You may need to learn to switch your work ethic to another channel so you can receive more pleasure for *yourself* during your sexual interactions. And contradictory as it sounds, you may actually need to work hard to convince yourself that sexual play is possible and permissible for you (see the permission-giving exercises in Chapter 1).

> **REMEMBER** Sexual safety means having fun—and taking care of Number One.

## *Initiating Play*

How is it possible for women to assert themselves both playfully and safely at the same time? Women talk about these essentials—maybe you can add some of your own:

- Seduction
- Flooding the senses
- Inventiveness
- Teasing without frustrating

Here are some conversational gambits women have told us get things rolling.

1. **The fine art of seduction:** This is the invitation to the dance; encouragement without aggressiveness. Do you know Margie Adam's wonderful song: "Would You Like to Tap-dance on the Moon with Me?" Well, try one of the following phrases, or substitute something of your own:

"Would you like to run along the beach with me...build a sandcastle...fly a kite...tell your last night's dream?"

"Come and ride a tilt-a-whirl with me...march in a parade ...watch the fireworks...climb an apple tree..."

2. **Flooding the senses:** Hopefully your partner will get the hint and do the same for you next time. If this doesn't happen, and if you find yourself continually giving, even if you ask, then that ceases to be play and becomes hard work. It might be time to reconsider the relationship. In any event, the point of flooding the senses is to find ways to appeal to sight, touch, hearing, smell, and taste to make a relationship between the two of you quite irresistible:

"While you lie here on this fur rug by the fire listening to Ravel's 'Bolero,' I will peel and feed you grapes, massage your chest with warmed almond oil, blow softly into your left ear, knead each finger lovingly, rub your feet with salt and then rinse them in rosewater."

3. **Inventiveness:** This is to turn up your partner's thermostat by using surprise, humor, art, music, cooking—any talents you can muster:

"Let's sit in total darkness and sing together."

"Let's sit back to back and play telephone. We can tell each other our secret sexual longings."

"Let's draw Kitty's tail slowly across the insides of our elbows."

4. **Teasing without frustrating:** This means coming on without copping out. It means encouraging your partner to think lusty and just slightly bawdy thoughts in the interests of mutually developing your P.Q. (playfulness quotient):

"Let me show you my X-rated corner. In it, you'll find a number of items, which we can use in any way our imaginations devise.

"There are fur mitts, a red silk scarf, a sequined Lone-Ranger mask. And there are feathers of various sorts, especially peacock feathers and snowy ostrich plumes."

## A Note about Sexual Goals

Teaching your partner to be more sexually playful may lead both you and your partner to orgasm. There are many safe ways to orgasm, ways that do not involve the exchange of body fluids. You might want to review earlier chapters to remind yourself of some of these ways.

Also, playfulness may lead you or your partner to desire intercourse. If you feel that intercourse is not a safe activity, there are many alternatives for sexual satisfaction. Again, you might want to review earlier chapters to remind yourself of these.

Let's listen to some stories of women who've learned to be playful without abandoning responsibility for their own lives. These women describe five ways they can take charge of their own sexual enjoyment in absolute safety, and teach their partners the joys of play: out-of-bed encounters, dressing and undressing, smelling good, toying with food, and using erotica.

Maybe you can use these ideas to teach your partner some new tricks.

## Out-of-Bed Encounters

First, women can be inventive about where they make love. Getting out of bed, and out of the bedroom, is a great way to begin the teaching process with your partner. In fact, for some women, the path to ecstasy starts here. Researchers are aware of this, too. In her book *Shared Intimacies,* Barbach mentions that variety of scene was a turn-on for many of the women she interviewed. In the 1977 *Redbook* survey, three out of every four married women varied the location of their lovemaking to make it more exciting. *Loving Women,* by the Nomadic Sisters, suggests a number of settings that make sexual experiences more exciting, and tells us that one of their authors has tried it on top of a refrigerator: "...can be risky, but fun!"

This is not to downgrade in-bed sex. The comfort, security, and familiarity of home and bed are hard to beat, and having their own pillow and security blanket is essential to some women's experiences of satisfaction. But for many women, getting out of bed has some of the benefits of taking a vacation: changed routine, experimentation, and, above all, excitement.

Out-of-bed romps may be good for teaching pleasure, but what makes them a technique for safety? It is primarily intercourse that puts women at risk, and most of the women who talked with us mentioned no push toward the usually expected sexual goal of intercourse during their out-of-bed encounters. Intercourse may occur, but it isn't the aim of the encounter. The aim is sensuous surprise.

Sometimes the surprise is not entirely welcome. We know a woman who filled her bathtub with cherry Jell-O as a birthday treat to play out a long-time fantasy: "It didn't gel and was disgustingly sticky, but we laughed so hard and had so much fun, we felt as close as if we'd just had mad, passionate sex."

Other women thrilled to the danger of out-of-bed discovery, especially in moving vehicles. When we asked why being on the road seems to incite sexual exploration, one woman suggested maybe this is because we get so much basic training during adolescence in the back seats of cars. She said we ought to title this phenomenon "auto" eroticism.

We know women who have initiated escapades in trains, buses, airplanes, and canoes as well as cars, and one woman claims she made love on a bicycle (she doesn't say how). And then there was Katya, who drove cross-country in a camper that jauntily displayed on its door a wood-burned sign that advertised:

*If this van's a-rockin'*
*Don't bother knockin'*

For many women, making love outdoors, amidst nature, enhances sexual feelings and also a sense of spiritual connectedness with a partner. These women talk about picnics in the grass ("So green and sweet"), rolling down sand dunes in a full-body hug ("Like moon-wrestling"), the shadowy romance of caressing each other's faces by a midnight fire in the snow ("We'd just seen *Dr. Zhivago*").

For some women, water is a favorite. Whether in pond, creek, or ocean, underwater kisses taste spectacular, according to women who love them. "Cool and raspberry-flavored," says one woman, "like the ultimate ice cream cone."

Another woman told us about cavorting in the ocean waves with her lover: "We felt like porpoises, tumbling over one another in the surf and shrieking with laughter. Every once in a while we'd slide over each other's bodies with our slippery, wet skin and pretend to fertilize each other."

**HOT TIP** For outdoor romps, remember bug spray and something to put between you and the ground, like a blanket or poncho. Nothing quenches the fire of passion quite so fast as swarming gnats or muddy bottoms. Aficionados keep outdoor supplies at the ready in the trunks of their cars.

And, just in case your out-of-bed episode does include intercourse, make sure you bring along your safe-sex equipment: condoms, spermicide, and any other paraphernalia you feel would be helpful. Spontaneity is nice, but playing safe can help you live, and love, to a happy old age.

## *Dressing and Undressing*

Another way women can teach their partners to play is with makeup, body decoration, jewelry, and clothing. These can be extremely erotic in and of themselves, and for some women, and men, the acts of dressing and undressing can rival any other kind of sexual stimulation. Moreover, like changing the scene, they can help women take charge of their sexual encounters and have fun safely without assuming a goal of intercourse.

It's important to point out that we're advocating freedom

of expression in adorning your body and are in no way suggesting that you "doll up" to meet someone else's dress or makeup codes, or that you cover your body because someone else is ashamed of your nudity or finds your body inadequate.

In fact, sometimes you can send out more interesting messages with just the right clothes on than you can when you're naked. Some women like to dress for fun, for the shock value, or for the excitement it creates for their partners.

One woman relates: "One of my most electric experiences took place in a French restaurant. Heads turned as I squeezed past the tables, and when my partner saw me coming he lit up just like a pinball machine. He agrees that the Evening of the Dress ranks as one of the hottest we ever spent, even though we never finished off the evening by rushing off to bed. Tantalizing each other over the oysters was more gratifying, and much more memorable."

Christine, who owns a boutique for women, talked with us about makeup and body decoration: "Somewhere along the line I figured out that ever since ancient times women have decorated themselves to feel good, and also to attract mates. I figure if they could do it, and if monkeys and birds can flash their colors when they feel sexy, why can't I?

"So I wear colorful makeup when I want to send out certain messages. It's a tremendous turn-on for my husband, and it's made him much more tuned in to my signals. Really, it's broadened the definition of sex for both of us—way beyond intercourse and even flirtation to something intensely playful. I gave him a body-painting kit for his birthday, and we finger-painted each other with blue feathers and great silver wings. Now I know how Leda felt when she was mounted by a swan!"

Bear in mind, too, that tastes vary, and not all women are turned on by decorating themselves. Many prefer their sex play *au naturel* and tell us they dress mainly for the pleasure of taking it off: "When I'm with my partner, I want to be simple and direct and naked. Then my body belongs to me. I feel safe and sensual. Adding crotchless panties and little black nighties complicates things for me. I get competitive and begin to role-play. I can't imagine having a great sexual experience other than naked."

## *Smelling Good*

We develop our natural ability to smell as soon as we're born, to help guide us to the nourishment and pleasure of our mother's breasts. But as soon as we stop being cuddly little infants, smell is a sense we're taught to ignore, at least as it applies to body odors. In our culture, the way we treat body smell is through deception and disguise. Americans spend millions of dollars each year first to remove natural odors, then millions more to smell of something else, like a meadow, a tiger, a garden, or Paris.

Fooling the sense of smell like this takes away one of our great sources of pleasure and forces us to disconnect from an essential part of our remembered experience and our present potential. This may be especially true for women: Scientists tell us that women have more highly developed sensitivity than men because our ability to smell is linked to our menstrual cycles.

Some of the women who have talked with us say that smell is indeed a primary erotic turn-on for them. Being able to fully enjoy their sense of smell awakens their awareness of other senses as well. These women agree that overcoming societal taboos and rules about smells is one of the ways they can be assertive in their sexual encounters and treat themselves to the full spectrum of all their senses. Moreover, women can use their usually superior sense of smell to encourage men to notice a sensory world they may not have even been aware of.

*And smelling is safe. No one has ever yet gotten STDs from sniffing.*

Andrea spoke to us of a special recipe for comfort she has with her partner: "When I really need to know he's *there* for me, sometimes I just shamelessly snuffle him all over, like a puppy. He used to think it was really weird, but now it's become an affirming act for both of us.

"I notice how he has all sorts of different smells. The creases in his neck are a whole other landscape from his chest hairs. And his ears always seem to smell wild and sweet, like the outdoors. When we kiss, his breath makes me remember when we first met. It moves me to tears. It can even move me to orgasm. I love his smell so much I've been wondering how I could possibly bottle it."

But women can be repelled by smells, too, not just the almost universal turn-offs like liquor and cigarettes on the breath, but products that are designed to enhance sexual pleasure. Andrea continues: "When we were experimenting once, we tried one of those strawberry-flavored ointments. It was gross, like five-fruit bubble gum, not sexy at all. I turn on to his own natural self, not to deodorant, and certainly not to some fake strawberry cover-up."

Smell is the sense that's most likely to evoke memories, and women mentioned all kinds of nostalgic associations they had with certain smells. Susan relates: "Oddly enough, the smell of lavender water is one of the most sensuous experiences for me. I connect it with my grandmother, who loved me and accepted me utterly. It's erotic, because being around her made me feel so alive and full of myself. Another erotic smell? The first spring whiff of new grass. It brings on the rush of first love. It's an unfailing aphrodisiac."

If you're like Susan and Andrea, your nose is a built-in pleasure-enhancer that you can use at will to make any enjoyable sexual encounter even more enjoyable. And you can have the added satisfaction of bringing your partner along with you. Here are some of the ways women suggest you might use smelling good to enhance your sexual and sensual perceptions and teach your partner to enjoy more sensuous playfulness:

- Dab on some perfume or light a stick of incense to evoke specific feelings (not to fool the senses by disguising natural smells).
- Add a drop or two of "essential oil" to the unscented massage oil or lotion you use on one another. Try musk or almond or sandalwood (you can buy them in little vials at your health-food store); your skin will reward you for hours.
- Scent your sheets with sachets or herbs. You can also tuck some of these in your closets and drawers so your clothes can help you feel sensual all day long.

- And remember, you are what you eat. A healthy diet, along with no smoking or heavy drinking, will help keep your breath and body odors sweet and sexy. This will go a long way in helping both you and your partner to disobey your antisniff training about each other's natural odors.

## *Toying with Food*

Taking charge of food isn't something that's new to women. We've been cooks and serving maids throughout history, and that creates a special problem now for some of the women who've talked with us. Preparing food may hold conflicts because of its associations with three-meal-a-day drudgery.

But other women are able to recognize that food presents one of life's great opportunities for play, nurturing and deep-down satisfaction. They also recognize that, along with being servants, women have been wise to the erotic uses of food since the beginning of time. After all, when Cleopatra asked to have a grape peeled for her, she was not just thinking of a between-meal treat.

Food lovers of today don't have to engage in Cleopatra's dangerous power games, though. Women can use food for arousal without risk. They can enjoy—and teach—each aspect of planning, preparation and consumption as its own safe encounter.

### Collecting Recipes

Edie tells us: "I love food. And I love to talk about it almost as much as I love to eat it. My partner and I are waiting out our AIDS tests, and before we have intercourse with one another, we're flirting with food instead.

"Our present hobby is collecting recipes on how to bake bread that looks like every body part you ever wanted to nibble on. Of course, it has to taste good, too. Our favorite so far is a cinnamon swirl torso decorated with chocolate lips. Sometimes we think we'd rather keep on playing with food than have sex.

In fact, our fantasy is to institute an Erotic Foods Bake-Off right here in our home town."

## Shopping

You can keep it simple. Leave the soup-to-nuts school of food shopping behind. For example, try losing yourself in the produce section of your supermarket. Those giant refrigerated bins can turn into veritable pleasure chests if you allow your erotic imagination to play. And if you take your partner along, you can engage in some sex education and outright flirtation as you consider together the pleasurable uses of mangoes and peaches or a well-shaped carrot, zucchini, or cucumber.

**HOT TIP** Joan, a sexologist, asked that we offer the following personal advice on veggies: "Now that you've discovered the erotic uses of the contents of your refrigerator's vegetable hydrator, I want to issue a warning. Make sure you bring the icy darlings to room temperature before you use them or you may be in for a shock. Also, wash them thoroughly, and don't share them any more than you would share condoms or sex toys."

## Presentation

Here, the possibilities are endless. Let the recipe and the situation dictate your style.

Are you offering a subtle selection of perfectly shaped whole, raw carrots as an in-bed treat? Perhaps arrange them in a star pattern on a lace doily. Or ask your lover to present you with a shiny green cucumber tucked in a lettuce-colored silk scarf.

Have you created a succulent Middle Eastern dinner? You and your partner can arrange it on a huge tray and savor it while sitting cross-legged on an oriental rug (or any kind of rug). This way, you can talk about all the things you could do together in 1,001 nights, and then choose whether or not it's appropriate for you to act them out. Or to fine-tune your senses, drape yourselves in flowing robes and try an Indian curry outside in summer, just as dusk is falling and the night sounds are coming up.

A selection of frosty, cut-up fruits can be enhanced by serving them with your best silver spoons. You can eat out of the same bowl and use the opportunity to make eye contact and engage in any other safe flirtations that this particular meal and partner suggest.

## Eating

Miss Manners gave us one sort of food etiquette. Your erotic imagination can give you another.

Fingers were made before forks, and finger eating has an etiquette all its own. You can make it up as you go along. Succulent treats like artichokes and asparagus beckon you to use fingers, and dishes like steamed clams and corn on the cob may cry out for you to dig in right up to your elbows.

Eating can be a preamble to lovemaking. "In fact, eating can be lovemaking," says one of our reporters. "Remember that great scene in *Tom Jones* when they're feeding each other dinner, and all the juices are running down their chins and arms? Well, try feeding your lover a lobster. Or a pomegranate or mango. Or even a peeled banana."

## Sensuous Spreads

Some women have taken a giant step with food by using it *on* the body. The advantage here is that you can have an outlandish experience—far away from body fluids, genitals, and unsafe sex.

Here's Julia's recipe for turning your partner into a Fourth-of-July strawberry shortcake:

1. Slather the torso with whipped cream (you can steer clear of the genitals and still produce a splendid effect). Julia says

she likes to use real cream, but you can also use the spray-can variety. The pressurized spray tickles when it hits your skin, and some people like that.

2. Decorate with strawberries, whole or halved. You can use other fruits in season. Raspberries and peaches are especially delectable (the voice of experience tells us that blueberries tend to roll off and stain the sheets and generally aren't worth the bother). The decorations must be completed quickly and deftly before the whipped cream begins to run.

3. Voilà! Your shortcake is ready. Start anywhere, and lick and slurp to your heart's content. The more actively you go at it, the faster you'll burn off some of those calories in the whipped cream.

Julia adds a note here that if you don't care about having an absolutely traditional Fourth of July, you can drizzle a little chocolate sauce or Amaretto over the whole concoction. If you're on a health kick, or trying to stay away from dairy products, you can skip the whipped cream altogether.

This kind of food play is a preamble to much licking, sucking, and laughter. And it's also a preamble to a sensuous bath or shower, for these spreads may be sexy, but they're also sticky.

## *Enjoying Erotica*

Researchers and psychologists have told us that women are not turned on to sexual imagery to the same degree as men. But if you think about it yourself, and talk to enough women, you discover that this may be far from true. First of all, studies these professionals are citing are based on women's reactions to commercial pornography, that is, pictures, stories, and films that focus on men's satisfaction, and on women reveling in the role of sex objects. Often the women are also depicted as the objects of some kind of violence. This macho show of sex is of course going to leave most women at the starting gate.

We classify this kind of sexual imagery as unsafe sex because it subordinates women in order to create sexual arousal in viewers and readers: Rape, battering, and psychological abuse affect more women than AIDS or other STDs.

But there's another kind of sexual imagery that turns women on—or so say the thousands of clients, students, friends, and colleagues we've talked with in the last twenty years. There is a broader imagery than the macho kind, one that encompasses tender emotional feelings as well as physical sensation. It's both pleasure-enhancing and perfectly safe.

We believe that enjoying such sexual imagery offers a special chance for women to add dimension to their sex lives and to experience the sensation of being in control, safely taking charge and having fun, during sex.

Moreover, through safe imagery, women can introduce their partners to another kind of erotic awareness—soft, soulful, and sexy. These are quite different images from the pornography they might pick up in the corner magazine store. Sharing women's erotica is a chance to expand your partner's sexual imagination and also offer a vivid contrast to commercial porn, perhaps making it obvious that most commercial porn is not really so very sexy after all.

What is this safe imagery? Women have reported enjoying Friday's books on fantasy, *My Secret Garden* and *Forbidden Flowers*. Barbach has edited two books of women's erotica, *Pleasures* and *Erotic Interludes*. And there's the Kensington Ladies Erotica Society, a group of California housewives who got together to tell each other their favorite and sexiest stories. Their delightful books are named *Ladies' Own Erotica* and *Look Homeward, Erotica*. Tee Corinne's photographs in *Yantras of Woman Love* reframe our erotic view of women's bodies.

You can eroticize almost anything safely. Pornography is, after all, only an attitude, one way of looking at things. As long as you think about the world in terms of domination, your images are going to be manipulative, as is your sex. But if you think about the world in terms of tender and interdependent relationships, even in terms of wild passion, all sorts of things can become erotic.

One of the women we talked with summed it up: "I think nature is one long X-rated film. Have you ever watched a storm over the sea, or dragonflies having an in-flight affair? Or noticed how tenderly each nasturtium leaf holds a drop of water after a rain? To me these feel much more sexy than two people going at each other in bed with buggy whips."

Inventing your own erotica is a challenge and a splendid way to teach your partner to play. Here are four activities recommended by women who've tried them:

- Train your eyes to be unashamed about looking at both men and women, and talk about your experiences with your partner. If you're confirmed body-watchers, you can have a number of safe encounters just walking to the grocery store—and even more sexual enjoyment running the replays with each other.
- Write your own erotic fantasies, and encourage your partner to do the same. The act of writing can be an encounter in itself. That's how the Kensington Ladies got their start.
- Choose fantasies to read aloud together.
- Enact scenes from your fantasies. Let your imagination dance freely. If you like, you can dress for the part. For kicks, and some deeper understanding of each other, try reversing roles with your partner.

## *Playing with Fire: Booze, Grass, Coke, Poppers, and Ground Unicorn Horn*

We hope you will find ways to get delightfully high on some of the safe-sex practices outlined in this book. But there are some substances that don't mix with safe sex. These are substances women may need to steer clear of and encourage their partners not to play with as well.

Alcohol and marijuana are both central nervous system depressants. This means that they slow down the normal checks and balances on your limbic system, the part of the brain that dictates your level of emotion and sexual arousal. That's why having a drink or smoking pot may release your inhibitions enough to allow you to enjoy great sex. In this sense, these substances can be welcome breakers of sexual ice and can even have an aphrodisiac effect.

But these substances can also cut off your capacity to think clearly. They can alter perception of time, fuzz priorities, and limit ability to speak logically and sensibly. In other words, as alcohol and marijuana remove your sexual inhibitions, they can also lead you to say and do things you might regret in the morning (if you even remember you've said and done them). They certainly don't help you take charge of practicing safe sex. And they can short out the signals that allow sex to register as lasting satisfaction.

Cocaine is a feel-good drug, a chemical stimulant that directly affects the brain and mimics the sensations produced by sexual stimulation. This is also true of its free-based form, crack. In fact, cocaine is the only drug that's as powerful a stimulant as sex, and its high can feel like a sexual high and even become confused with it. Last night's great sex, or great partner, might be nothing more than last night's snort of coke, or drag of crack—and perhaps the beginning of a life-threatening habit.

Amyl nitrite and butyl nitrite are also marketed as sex enhancers. They are sold in sex shops as "poppers" or under brand names like "Rush" and "Locker Room." They dilate the blood vessels, intensify orgasm, and give you a buzz, sending a sudden flushing to face and head. But although they may produce a flare of pleasure, they are potentially dangerous, and we do not recommend their use. They increase heart rate and decrease blood pressure, which can lead to heart problems or exacerbate existing heart problems.

Other mood-altering substances used to enhance sexual experiences include caffeine, sugar, and chocolate—all uppers. *Use them in moderation.* Whether these come in the form of a cup of coffee, a soda, a candy bar, or a scoop of ice cream, you need to be aware that they are actually little time bombs and can be just as addictive as alcohol or any other drug.

Studies show that caffeine, sugar, and chocolate can raise havoc with the immune system, and keeping your immune system in good shape is one of your first lines of defense against contracting the AIDS virus, as well as other STDs like chlamydia and herpes. And, just like alcohol, any of the mood alterers mentioned above can throw your mind into a state of confusion, blurring your safe-sex judgment and your willingness and ability to act in your own best interests.

**REMEMBER** At least 10 percent of condom failures are due to pilot error. If you love yourself and your partner, keep your wits about you when you're making love. Don't use mood-altering substances before or during sex, anymore than you would drink and drive.

## *Saying Yes to Pleasure and No to Unsafe Sex*

In preparation for shifting gears to the Question-and-Answer section of this book, let's review the major points about prevention, pleasure, and responsibility, and suggest a Safe-Sex Bill of Rights you can adapt for your personal situation.

### Prevention

Current media thinking models itself on a deprivation economy and offers three major options for safe sex: condom use, sexual abstinence, or permanent, absolute monogamy.

Each of these options has its catch 22: Condom use offers some protection but is risky at best. Sexual abstinence may keep you from getting AIDS but may trigger other health problems, including depression and anxiety. Permanent monogamy may be fine in theory, but in fact, more women and men break their vows of fidelity than keep them.

No movement in history has yet been able to stop everybody from being sexual or from having multiple partners. But with our advanced communication techniques, we have a chance, and a responsibility, to educate our whole population about replacing dangerous sexual habits with safe ones.

For women, safe sex means more than AIDS prevention, and it certainly means more than just learning how to use spermicide and insist on condom use, although these can be vitally important if you're having genital intercourse with a partner you're not 100 percent sure of. Safe sex means self-knowledge and the ability to choose safe partners and safe activities. This means coming to terms with two concepts that have been left out of the vocabulary of many women: pleasure and responsibility.

## The Pleasure Factor

Coming to terms with pleasure means allowing yourself to play. This is an essential step toward the effective practice of sexual safety. It enables you to consider all the delightful things you can do safely, rather than seeing safe sex only as deprivation and interruption of spontaneity. Moreover, when you can understand and accept your whole constellation of needs and desires, the emotional and spiritual ones as well as the needs and desires of your body, you have established the basis for deep and loving communication with your partner.

Opting for sexual pleasure does not necessarily mean rebelling against authority, nor does it mean denying responsibility. It means accepting that your well-being is as important as your partner's. In the age of AIDS and other STDs, sexual pleasure means active participation in all phases of your sexual experience, from communicating your needs and desires, to giving and receiving stimulation that feels good, to practicing scrupulously safe sex.

We have consistently challenged the view that the main reason for sexual pleasure is to reach orgasm. In fact, we've challenged the traditional, goal-oriented view of sex. Over the years, many women have reported to us that a goal of intercourse, with a further goal of orgasm, may actually inhibit their pleasure. The intercourse goal has already put many women at risk in this age of AIDS and other STDs, and it has also carried with it the risk of pregnancy.

## The Responsibility Factor

Coming to terms with responsibility for your own sexuality means understanding with utter clarity this simple truth: *Refusal to practice safe sex is a form of sexual abuse.* It's self-abuse if you knowingly have unprotected sex with an infected partner; it's partner abuse if you or your partner is infected and fails to tell, or insists on having sex anyway.

Being responsible for yourself means you have power. It means you don't have to be either a perpetrator of unsafe sex or a victim of it. It means you do whatever it takes to learn how to choose partners who are responsive to your well-being. And it means you learn how to communicate your needs and desires.

Ultimately, safe sex boils down to being able to say Yes to pleasure and No to sex that is unsafe—emotionally, physically, spiritually.

The details of personal safety are an individual matter, but there *are* rights every woman should be able to count on in every single sexual situation.

We offer here a Bill of Rights for your sexual well-being and urge you to add to it to make it fit *you*.

Keep it in a convenient place and refer to it often.

Show it to your partner, and remember, *only a partner who respects your rights is a safe partner for you.*

### *My Safe-Sex Bill of Rights*

1. I have a right to my own body, and all of its sensations, including pleasure and pain.
2. I have a right to think my own thoughts, whatever they may be.
3. I have a right to feel the full spectrum of my own emotions: excitement, joy, and anger; sorrow and depression; love and fear. And I have a right to feel these whether or not my feeling them is acceptable to others.
4. I have a right to acknowledge my memories, whether they're of delight or abuse, and a right to base present sexual decisions on my memories.
5. I have a right to be sexual at all ages and stages of my life, and a right to choose how I define my sexuality, how I wish to express it, and with whom.
6. I have a right to expect that my sexual partner respect my body, thoughts, emotions, and general well-being—and a right to insist on respect for these, if necessary.
7. I have a right to ask for what I want.
8. I have a right to say No to any sexual encounter that feels unsatisfying or threatening at any time, whether physically, emotionally, or spiritually.
9. I have a right to say Yes to pleasure that's physically, emotionally, and spiritually safe.
10. I have a right to feel good about saying Yes and No, and a right not to feel fear, guilt, or obligation.

# SAFE-SEX ROAD MAP FOR CHAPTER 6: INTEGRATING PLEASURE AND RESPONSIBILITY

In Chapter 6 you've read what other women say about having fun during their sexual encounters and teaching their partners to play. This Safe-Sex Road Map is to help you discover more about how *you* feel and respond.

The Personal Response Chart at the end of this chapter is a self-assessment checklist for various kinds of sexual play: out-of-bed encounters, dressing and undressing, smelling good, toying with food, and enjoying erotica. Some of these categories may not be relevant for you, and there may be others you want to add.

We urge you to have fun with this chart. That way you can use it as a rehearsal for a safe sexual encounter.

You can fill it out as we suggest, or, if that reminds you too much of a ninth-grade personality test, you can write comments or poems on it or decorate it with psychedelic designs (which may remind you of tenth grade).

If charts are a total turn-off for you, here are two other suggestions that might bring results.

**1.** Draw a picture or cartoon of yourself taking charge and having fun. Use as much color as you like, and be sure to include all the safe-sex details that are important for you.

Play with it. One woman filled an oversized piece of paper with alabaster urns of spermicide and condoms that looked like angelfish with come-on expressions and wavy fins.

**2.** Write a soap opera starring yourself taking charge and having fun. Embellish it with all you've got, emphasizing safe-sex paraphernalia and actions.

A variation on this theme is to recite this "soap" into a tape recorder and play it back for yourself and your partner, choosing perfect timing of course.

If you elect to fill out the chart below, simply describe your experiences using the journalistic headings What, Where, When, How, and With Whom. Rate the experiences on a 1-to-10 scale, for both safety and pleasure.

However you decide to play with this Safe-Sex Road Map, we hope you can use it to more fully understand how you can have both initiative and enjoyment in your sexual encounters.

## Personal Response Chart: Taking Charge and Having Fun

| | *Safety Rating, 1–10* | *Pleasure Rating, 1–10* | *What* | *Where* | *When* | *How* | *With Whom* |
|---|---|---|---|---|---|---|---|
| **Out-of-Bed Encounters:** | | | | | | | |
| Indoors | | | | | | | |
| Outdoors | | | | | | | |
| Underwater | | | | | | | |
| Other | | | | | | | |
| **Dressing and Undressing:** | | | | | | | |
| Lingerie | | | | | | | |
| Clothing | | | | | | | |
| Jewelry | | | | | | | |
| Makeup | | | | | | | |
| Body decoration | | | | | | | |
| Other | | | | | | | |
| **Smelling Good:** | | | | | | | |
| Incense | | | | | | | |
| Perfumes | | | | | | | |
| Oils | | | | | | | |
| Body odors | | | | | | | |
| Other | | | | | | | |
| **Toying with Food:** | | | | | | | |
| Shopping | | | | | | | |
| Presentation | | | | | | | |
| Eating | | | | | | | |

(*continued*)

**Personal Response Chart: Taking Charge and Having Fun** (*Continued*)

| | *Safety Rating, 1–10* | *Pleasure Rating, 1–10* | *What* | *Where* | *When* | *How* | *With Whom* |
|---|---|---|---|---|---|---|---|
| Being fed | | | | | | | |
| Sensuous spreads | | | | | | | |
| Veggie dildos | | | | | | | |
| Other | | | | | | | |
| **Enjoying Erotica:** | | | | | | | |
| Reading | | | | | | | |
| Writing | | | | | | | |
| Looking | | | | | | | |
| **Haven't tried yet but would like to** | | | | | | | |

## *Personal Safe-Sex Commitment*

To make my sex life safer, I commit myself to doing the following about learning to play and teaching my partner to play:

________________________________________________________

________________________________________________________

________________________________________________________

________________________________________________________

## *My Follow-Up Safe-Sex Commitment*

Use this space to review and copy the safe-sex commitments you made at the ends of Chapters 1 to 5, so that you can see them all together in front of you and have a clear notion of all the things you've decided to do to increase the safety of your sexual encounters.

Star* the ones you feel are most necessary for you to put into practice right away.

Double-star** the ones that have the potential of turning you on.

## *Difficult Safe-Sex Commitments*

Safe sex is a relatively new concept, and you may have to initiate certain actions by yourself, without much help from a partner, and sometimes in the face of resistance from a partner. There may be some commitments you've made that you feel will be difficult for you to put into actual practice, however necessary they may be to your well-being.

*Write these difficult commitments in the space below.* Next to each one, state when you're going to begin, and how. For instance, if one of the difficult commitments you write down is "Asking Bill to use condoms," you might add:

"Next time I see Bill," and

"I'm going to start by buying three different kinds, and then asking Bill to pick his favorite."

## *Safe-Sex Commitments to Start Now*

Review your safe-sex commitments, and write a third list. This may be the most important one of all: *These are the commitments I'm willing to start right away.*

Next to each commitment state when you're going to begin and how. For instance, if self-pleasuring is what you write down, you might say: "Tonight—starting with a long, delicious bath."

# PART TWO

## Facts at Your Fingertips

# CHAPTER 7

# *Answers to Questions about AIDS and Other STDs*

This chapter addresses questions women may have about AIDS and other sexually transmitted diseases (STDs), as well as questions about the relative safety of specific sexual behaviors. We hope the question-and-answer format will help you find answers easily.

The facts about AIDS and other STDs are based on the latest data from the federal Centers for Disease Control. New findings on testing, treatment, and research are being reported daily; therefore, you need to understand that the information presented here is the latest available at the time of writing.

No matter what new findings emerge, however, the basic precepts of this book remain valid: Women can no longer afford to engage in unprotected intercourse, and women can learn to be responsible for the safe and pleasurable expression of their sexuality.

## *The Who, What, When, Why, and How of AIDS*

### *What is AIDS?*

The acronym AIDS stands for Acquired Immunodeficiency Syndrome.

*Acquired* means you don't inherit it genetically, like the color of your eyes and hair. It's something you get after you're conceived.

*Immunodeficiency* means that your immune system—the body's defense against disease—isn't working. The white blood cells—the front line of the system—are too weak or too few to fight off disease.

*Syndrome* refers to a group of symptoms, any or all of which are present when a person has a disease. The symptoms of AIDS include the infections and cancers you're unable to defend yourself against because the virus has destroyed part of your body's immune system.

### *How long has AIDS been around?*

AIDS is thought to have originated in Africa thirty to fifty years ago. The virus may have first appeared in monkeys, or it may have first appeared in human beings. Wherever it started, it probably became as deadly as it is now through a series of mutations.

It was first recognized as a problem in the United States in 1981, but it has probably been here and in Europe since the 1970s.

The virus was first identified in two groups of people: gay men and IV drug users. It then began to be identified in recipients of blood transfusions. In 1985, the United States began screening donated blood for the presence of HIV.

### *What does HIV-infected mean?*

HIV stands for Human Immunodeficiency Virus, the virus that causes AIDS.

HIV-infected means that a person has been exposed to the virus and has developed or will develop antibodies against it.

Antibodies are formed by the body when it is exposed to certain antigens. Antigens are substances that are foreign to the body, such as bacteria or viruses. The body has many antibodies to many different antigens.

### *If I have the HIV antibody will I develop AIDS?*

This is not known at this time. Approximately 20 to 50 percent of people infected with HIV develop AIDS within five years.[1] The percentage may increase as more time passes. Most infected people have not developed any symptoms yet, and so appear to be outwardly healthy.

It's important for you to know that all people who are HIV-infected can *transmit* the disease, even if they show no symptoms themselves. It's estimated that there are 10 million HIV-infected people in the world[2] and that most of these are asymptomatic, that is, they have no symptoms of AIDS at this time.

### *What is ARC?*

ARC is the acronym for AIDS-Related Complex. This is a syndrome that usually precedes AIDS itself. People with ARC have persistent swollen glands in at least two sites other than the groin area. These swollen glands have no known cause.

When a person with ARC develops certain malignancies or opportunistic infections (infections that don't pose a threat to people with healthy immune systems), that person is classified as having AIDS.

### *So there is a spectrum of being HIV-infected?*

Yes, and the spectrum may change as researchers learn more about HIV. The Centers for Disease Control has already expanded the definition of AIDS to include some symptoms that were formerly classified as ARC.

At present, the spectrum looks like this:

HIV-positive but asymptomatic    ARC    AIDS
k————————————————————————l

Another way to visualize those who are HIV-infected is to think of an iceberg. The tip of the iceberg represents the people with AIDS. The rest represents all the people with ARC, plus those who have the HIV antibodies but don't have symptoms.

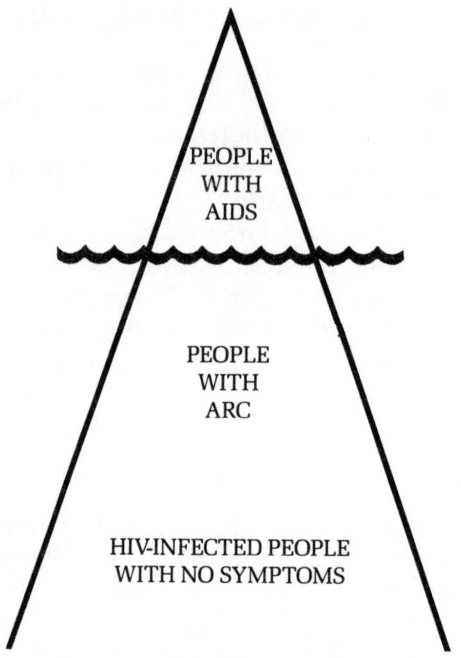


*The AIDS/ARC "Iceberg"*

***How would I know if I had AIDS?***

You'd probably experience the ARC symptoms described above. In addition to enlarged lymph nodes, you might have fatigue, weight loss, night sweats, diarrhea, a dry cough or difficulty breathing. You might also have persistent white spots in your mouth, and pink-to-purplish flat or raised blotches on your skin or mucous membranes.

At this writing, a diagnosis of AIDS is indicated when you have a positive HIV antibody test *and also* certain other diseases, such as HIV dementia, HIV wasting syndrome, or Kaposi's sarcoma, a cancer that attacks when your immune system has been weakened by HIV.

Even without a positive HIV antibody test, you can be diagnosed as having AIDS if you have *pneumocystis carinii* pneumonia (PCP), or if you're under 60 years old and have Kaposi's sarcoma (if you're over 60, Kaposi's sarcoma doesn't necessarily mean you have AIDS).

You may also experience forgetfulness, confusion, disorientation, and other signs of mental deterioration, which may occur by themselves or with other symptoms mentioned above.

### *Is there any way of telling exactly* when *I've been infected with the AIDS virus?*

Not at this time, although there are reports that shortly after infection, some people may have a prolonged feverish illness, something like mononucleosis.

### *Is there a vaccine for AIDS?*

Not yet. One of the reasons it's hard to find an effective vaccine for the AIDS virus is that the virus mutates rapidly; that is, it rearranges its structure. Also, it would be difficult to test a potential vaccine on laboratory rats, because they don't develop AIDS.

Despite these and other difficulties, scientists are working hard to find an effective vaccine.

### *Is there a cure for AIDS?*

Not yet. Although most STDs can be cured with a variety of antibiotics or antifungal medications, there are two STDs that can't be cured: herpes and AIDS.

### *Why can't herpes and AIDS be cured?*

There is no drug available to cure these diseases. They are both caused by viruses, and antibiotics do not kill viruses. The best way to control a viral disease is to find a vaccine and vaccinate those who are at risk of coming down with the illness, as has been done with polio, measles, and diphtheria.

### *What is the treatment for AIDS?*

There are antiviral drugs that prevent the virus from spreading and help restore some immune functions. These drugs have shown some clinical promise in prolonging the lives of certain AIDS patients. One of these drugs is azidothymidine (AZT). But AZT has a number of side effects. It also costs about $10,000 a year and must be taken for the rest of your life.

While scientists are working to develop other antiviral drugs as well as an effective vaccine, the best ways to control the spread of AIDS are education, testing, and counseling, and eliminating behaviors that exchange body fluids, especially blood and semen.

***Who can spread the virus? Can people who are HIV-infected spread it?***

Yes, these are the "healthy" carriers, who play the major role in the spread of AIDS. They may be infected for years without knowing it, and they may be transmitting the virus to others without knowing it. Once infected with the virus, a person may not have the symptoms of ARC or AIDS for ten or more years and may appear to be perfectly healthy.

***How is the AIDS virus transmitted or spread?***

HIV is a blood-borne virus that is spread from person to person. The virus is found in all body fluids, but its most compatible environments are blood and semen.

It is spread by four main methods:

1. **Sharing contaminated needles** A small amount of blood from an infected person may remain in the needle and syringe, and can be injected directly into the bloodstream of the next person using that needle and syringe.

   Users of illegal IV drugs are a major risk group because many of them share needles and syringes without proper sterilization. However, any unsterilized skin piercing, such as ear piercing or tattooing, can spread the disease from one person to another.

2. **Receiving contaminated blood or blood products** Prior to 1985, people may have received a unit of contaminated

blood or blood products. These transfusions of HIV-contaminated blood infected some of the recipients. For instance, many people with hemophilia who received blood developed AIDS.

An increasing number of countries, including the United States, are now screening donated blood and rejecting any blood that contains HIV antibodies.

3. **Mother to child** A mother with HIV antibodies has more than a 50 percent chance of spreading the virus to her unborn baby through the placenta, or via the birth canal while the baby is being born. It is also possible that she can transmit the virus through breastfeeding.

4. **Sexual intercourse and other sexual activity** The AIDS virus is present in semen, vaginal secretions, and other body fluids. It can be spread from man to man, man to woman, woman to man, and possibly woman to woman.

### *What do you mean by the term "safe sex"?*

We mean sensual pleasure, emotional pleasure, and physical activities that do not involve the exchange of body fluids. Our suggestions for safe-sex practices are in Chapters 1, 2, 3, 5, and 6.

### *What do you mean by the term "safer sex"?*

We mean using condoms and spermicides, also latex gloves or dental dams, to prevent the passage of body fluids from partner to partner. Our suggestions for safer-sex practices are in Chapter 4.

### *Can AIDS be transmitted by oral-genital sex?*

This is hard to document exactly, because it's hard to find people who practice only oral-genital sex. Consequently, researchers have conducted no definitive studies on the risks involved in oral-genital sex or in swallowing semen.

It's important to remember three things:

**1.** Any activity that results in the exchange of semen and blood, or vaginal fluid and blood, can theoretically transmit the AIDS virus. Therefore, bleeding gums, or any small tear or cut in the lining of the mouth or lips, could allow the virus to enter the body via semen, vaginal secretions, or menstrual blood.

**2.** There is less risk through oral-genital sex than through unprotected vaginal or anal intercourse, and swallowing semen is not as dangerous as direct blood-to-semen contact.

**3.** Unless you're absolutely sure you and your partner are free of the AIDS virus, use latex protection during oral-genital contact.

***Why is anal intercourse linked with the transmission of AIDS? And does this occur only with gay men?***

The lining of the rectum is thin, is easily torn, and may be particularly receptive to the AIDS virus. Anal intercourse (penis into rectum) can therefore result in direct infection, and is in fact one of the riskiest of all sexual activities.

Gay men may engage in anal intercourse with male partners; heterosexual men may engage in anal intercourse with women partners; bisexual men may engage in intercourse with either. Because of the risks, we do not recommend anal intercourse. But if this is a sexual activity you choose, use condoms, lubricated externally with a water-soluble lubricant, such as K-Y Jelly, unless you're absolutely sure both you and your partner are free of the AIDS virus.

***Is there any way that HIV is not spread?***

The AIDS virus is not spread through casual contact. That means it's not spread through coughing or sneezing, trying on clothes, or being near people in school or on the job. You can't get it in a swimming pool or hot tub. It's not spread by toilet seats, handshakes, hugs, closed-mouth kissing, telephones, contact sports, or food handlers in restaurants.

### *Can it be spread by mosquito bites?*

Although the AIDS virus has been found in the blood of mosquitoes, there have been no reported cases of AIDS being spread by mosquitoes.

### *Is it safe to donate blood?*

Yes. You cannot get AIDS by donating blood. Although needles are used to draw your blood, the needles are sterile.

### *Is it safe to receive blood transfusions today?*

If you have a blood transfusion, the likelihood of your being infected by the AIDS virus is small in the United States today.

Since 1985, blood donors have been routinely screened by interviews, and blood is not accepted from high-risk individuals. However, it's been reported that, especially in big cities, some high-risk individuals sell their blood and don't tell interviewers about their high-risk behavior.

Donated blood is routinely tested for the AIDS virus. But there is still what is called a "window." That is, if a blood donor has recently been infected with the AIDS virus but has not yet developed the HIV antibodies, the blood will not test HIV-positive even though it carries the virus.

The best way to protect yourself from being infected with the AIDS virus during transfusions is to donate your own blood prior to surgery. In most areas (but not all), this blood will be given back to you as needed.

## *All about Testing*

This section answers specific questions about testing for the HIV antibody. It also addresses who should be tested, where you can be tested, and the importance of pre- and post-test counseling.

### *Tell me about the test for the HIV antibody.*

The test for the HIV antibody is done on a sample of your blood.

It cannot detect the antibody as soon as you have become infected with the virus. The test is effective only after the antibody is produced by your body. Reports say this period ranges from two weeks to six months, but in some instances, it may be much longer. This is the "window" described above. Researchers are now working on a test that will identify the virus itself, which will eliminate this window. As of this writing, this test is not available to the public.

The enzyme-linked immunosorbent assay (ELISA) method is the quickest and least expensive test, but it produces a relatively high number of false positives. That is why the ELISA is routinely repeated if the reading is positive.

The Western Blot test is more accurate and more expensive. It is used to confirm two positive ELISAs. There is a very high degree of accuracy from the results of an ELISA test backed by a Western Blot.

### *What is meant by a "false positive" and "false negative"?*

A false positive says you have antibodies when you do not. Such a reading can occur by picking up unrelated foreign proteins—for example, in women who have had a number of children or a number of blood transfusions. These women have been exposed to "foreign" cells in their blood.

False positives have also been reported to occur in alcoholics and in women on the birth control pill.

If you're in any of these groups and you test positive, you can be tested again to see if the tests were accurate, and you will be offered post-test counseling during this period.

A false negative says you're not infected when you are. This can result if you're tested too soon after exposure to the virus and your body has not yet had a chance to form the antibody.

### *To achieve accurate results, when should the test be done?*

The test should be done at least three months after your latest possible exposure to the virus. *This means no contact with a partner's body fluids, and no contact with contaminated needles for at least three months before the test.*

Researchers are now suggesting that the test be conducted a full six months after contact with the body fluids of another person or IV needles, and then repeated after still another six months.

***I've heard about some insurance companies dropping clients who test positive. Is that true?***

One of the major problems for people with AIDS is discrimination, and insurance is a case in point.

Some insurance companies refuse applicants once a positive test result is known, and some have been known to drop people just because they had the testing done. We advise that you don't submit the bill for your test to your insurance company unless you're sure the company won't discriminate.

***What about other discrimination?***

The military now tests new recruits and rejects those who test positive.

Employment discrimination is illegal, but it is also growing.

If you are considering being tested, be sure your anonymity is guaranteed (and do not give your name if you are asked). If you do give your name, be sure of confidentiality—make sure that your results will not be reported on your medical record or anywhere else.

***How is an "anonymous" test different from a "confidential" test?***

In an anonymous test, your name is never asked for nor recorded. Your blood is coded with a number, and you must use that number when you come, in person, to get your results.

In a confidential test, your name is recorded, but the test results and your name are kept private. Your physician can have access to confidential results if needed.

***I've heard that there are tests you can do at home to determine if you have the antibodies. Is this true?***

Yes, do-it-yourself AIDS antibody test kits are being developed by DuPont and Abbott. While these assure anonymity, one of the big problems we see with self-testing is that there is no counseling. An advantage of going to a testing center is that you receive pre-test and post-test counseling.

***Where can a person get HIV-antibody testing?***

Anonymous antibody testing is provided through the department of health in most states. Many county health clinics also provide testing. For information, call your state department of health or the national hot line number given in Chapter 9.

***I'm not homosexual, and I don't use IV drugs. Should I be tested?***

Only if you fall into one of the following groups:

- You've had more than three or four sexual partners a year.
- You're planning to become pregnant.
- You've had sexual contact in the last ten years with an HIV-positive person, someone who uses IV drugs, or someone who is bisexual.
- You've had sexual contact with a partner of any of these persons.
- You're a health-care worker who's been exposed to the body secretions of an AIDS patient.
- You had a blood transfusion before 1985, when blood screening began.
- You're sick, and your doctor recommends the test.
- You're concerned, and want to be tested.

# *Other Sexually Transmitted Diseases—Signs and Symptoms*

This section addresses specific questions about other sexually transmitted diseases, such as syphilis, gonorrhea, chlamydia, trichomonas, and herpes, that plague women and change their lifestyles.

### *Are there other sexually transmitted diseases that women should be concerned about?*

Yes. The most common STDs are AIDS, chlamydia, genital warts, gonorrhea, herpes, syphilis, vaginitis, viral hepatitis, trichomonas, and *Candida albicans*.

STDs are infectious diseases, caused by viruses, fungi, or bacteria, passed from person to person through intimate sexual contact. Over 10 million people in the United States get STDs every year.

If you have signs or symptoms listed in the chart on page 160, see your doctor or visit your health center immediately.

### *Are there high-risk groups for STDs?*

The high-risk groups include people who have multiple sex partners, homosexual and bisexual men, teenagers, prostitutes, IV drug users, sex partners of infected individuals, and people who do not practice safer-sex techniques.

It's crucial to bear in mind that people from all walks of life can get STDs, including AIDS. What causes STDs is *behavior*, not a person's politics, ethnic background, or sexual orientation.

> **REMEMBER** *Risk behaviors* are more relevant than *risk groups*. It isn't who you are that matters, it's what you do. As with AIDS, you're not protected just because you're not gay and don't use IV drugs. STDs can be transmitted sexually between men and women, in either direction.
>
> **PROTECT YOURSELF AND YOUR PARTNER**

## Other STDs—Signs and Symptoms

| | *Chlamydia* | *Genital warts* | *Gonorrhea* | *Herpes* | *Syphilis* | *Vaginitis* | *Viral hepatitis* | *Tricho-monas* | *Candida albicans* |
|---|---|---|---|---|---|---|---|---|---|
| Itching | | x | | | | x | | x | x |
| Nausea | x | | | | | | x | | |
| Painful urination | x | | x | x | | x | | | |
| Burning on urination | x | | x | x | | x | | | x |
| Abdominal pain | x | | x | | | | x | | |
| Vaginal discharge | x | x | x | x | | x | | x | x |
| Fatigue and fever | | | | x | | | | | |
| Skin changes and rashes | | x | | x | | | x | | |
| Sores on or near genitals | | | | x | x | | | | |

### *What about high-risk geographical locations?*

Not surprisingly, the highest concentration of people with AIDS and other STDs is in the big cities. This means that if you or your partner has had sexual partners from a metropolitan area, you might want to be tested, even though you're showing no signs or symptoms.

Having a blood transfusion in a big city may also be riskier than having one in a small town with no AIDS population.

## *Women and AIDS*

Women are the fastest growing risk group for AIDS in the United States. The questions and answers in this section deal with specific concerns women have about how they can keep themselves safe.

### *Aren't I pretty safe if I'm a woman? Isn't AIDS mainly a gay male disease?*

No. Although it's true that in the United States AIDS is currently more prevalent in the gay male community, it's now beginning to spread through heterosexual communities, too. And women need to know that the number of women infected with AIDS is growing faster than in any other population. As of this writing, there were more than three times as many women showing symptoms or testing HIV-positive than there were two years ago. In the Caribbean and in central Africa as many women as men are infected.

### *As a woman, just how concerned do I have to be?*

You need to know that AIDS is an epidemic with no end in sight. For instance, an International Communications Research Poll reported that AIDS is the United States's number-one health concern, followed by cancer and heart disease. In New York City, women who have contracted AIDS from heterosexual contact have been the city's fastest growing HIV-infected group since 1985; AIDS is the leading killer of women between the ages of 25 and 29,[3] the second for women 30 to 34, and the third for women 15 to 19.[4]

***Which women should be most concerned about contracting AIDS?***

Women who are at the greatest risk are:

- Women who use or have used IV drugs
- Women whose sex partners are at high risk or whose sex partners have had sex with someone at high risk (IV drug users, prostitutes, multiple sexual partners, gay or bisexual men)
- Women who have received contaminated blood products
- Health-care workers who handle the blood of AIDS patients

However, AIDS, like any other STD, can be spread by any partner, not just by people who are in obvious high-risk groups.

***Does this mean that women are now more vulnerable than men?***

Not necessarily. It is crucial to understand that you don't catch AIDS because of who you are. It doesn't matter how smart you are, how old, how well-off, or whether you're a man or a woman, gay or straight. You catch AIDS because of what you do.

***I've heard that the AIDS virus is pretty fragile. What kills it, and what environments does it like best?***

As we've said, you can't get AIDS from a drinking glass, a towel, or a toilet seat. The virus weakens and dies after it leaves the body and hits the air. It's also killed by common substances found in most households, such as alcohol, hydrogen peroxide, and ordinary household bleach in a solution of 1 part bleach to 9 parts water (of course, these are to be used externally only).

The environments the virus likes to travel in best are blood and semen. This means that the two riskiest things you can do are to share a hypodermic needle with someone who has the AIDS virus, and to have vaginal or anal intercourse without using a condom and a spermicide. And that's true whether you're a mother, a high school student, or a factory worker.

### *Can a woman transmit AIDS to a man?*

It's much more likely for a man to infect a woman or another man with the AIDS virus than it is for a woman to infect a man. However, cases have been reported in which a woman has transmitted the disease to a man. Menstrual blood or vaginal fluids might be the mode of transmission.

### *I'm a lesbian. Do I have to worry?*

Although lesbians are one of the lowest risk groups for AIDS, you may be at risk. Physicians and AIDS educators vary in their opinion about just how much you have to worry, but to put your question in perspective, consider the following:

- Your partner may have contracted the AIDS virus through a blood transfusion or through handling infected blood products.
- Your partner may have had sex with a male partner who spread the virus to her recently or years ago.
- Your partner may have contracted AIDS through sharing infected needles.
- Your partner may be HIV-positive without knowing it.

Any sexual behavior between two women in which there is oral, anal, or vaginal contact can spread the infection. Even though breast and vaginal secretions contain smaller concentrations of the AIDS virus than semen or blood (including menstrual blood), we advise that you use latex during contact with these parts of the body, unless you're absolutely sure of your partner (see Chapter 4 for details).

> **REMEMBER** *Unless you're absolutely sure you and your partner are free of the AIDS virus, you should practice safer-sex techniques, no matter which sex your partner is.*

### *My partner and I are heterosexual and don't practice anal intercourse. Am I still at risk?*

You are at risk if your partner is infected with the AIDS virus.

Aside from anal intercourse, researchers believe that penis-vagina intercourse is the major route of heterosexual transmission. Even if you do not have any small breaks in the skin in the genital area, the friction from the normal thrusting of intercourse can create or aggravate microscopic skin breaks.

You may not be able to see or feel minor injuries to the vaginal tissue. However, these tiny breaks in the tissue are exactly what the virus needs to reach the white blood cells that it attacks. Also, the longer you have sexual interactions with an infected partner, the greater your chances of becoming infected.

### *My best friend was raped. What are the chances she has AIDS?*

Only testing six months after the event can give an answer to your question.

AIDS has given a new dimension to the fact of rape for women of all ages, whether it is acquaintance rape, marital rape, or rape by a stranger. The risk of AIDS adds to the traumatic stresses your friend must face as a result of being sexually violated. In addition to being afraid of infection, she may feel dirty, guilty, angry, and terrified for a long time after the event. She may also feel worthless and depressed, but she needs your continued friendship, no matter how bad she feels about herself. And she may need specific support in many ways:

- Listening to her tell and retell the story of the rape
- Accepting her fears as real
- Encouraging her to express her rage
- Letting her know you don't blame her for what happened
- Helping her partner understand what she's going through
- Helping her find counseling, if need be
- Standing by her if she decides to report the rape and pursue legal action

### *I have night sweats and diarrhea. Do I have AIDS?*

Not necessarily. These are also symptoms of other diseases. But if you're concerned, see your health-care provider and have testing done to set your mind at rest.

Make sure the testing is anonymous or confidential, because fear of AIDS is causing discrimination. People who are tested may be at risk for losing their jobs or insurance coverage.

### *Why is there such a high incidence of AIDS among women in other countries such as African nations?*

This may be linked to unsanitary medical practices. Needles and syringes used for injections are not always sterilized between use on different patients. Also, blood transfusions are used more frequently than in the United States, and screening for the AIDS virus is not always done as it is in the United States.

Some sex researchers point out that the widespread practice of infibulation (sewing or otherwise closing shut the vagina) causes vaginal tissue to tear during intercourse, making it an easy host for the AIDS virus in semen. Infibulation also means that more couples use anal intercourse, and rectal tissue tears easily, making it an easy pathway for infection.

Further, there's a high incidence of other STDs in Africa, and the open sores of both syphilis and herpes provide entry points for the AIDS virus.

# *What about Pregnancy?*

In this section, we answer questions about pregnancy and artificial insemination.

Women should know two major facts about AIDS and pregnancy:

1. Pregnancy weakens your immune system and can increase your chances of developing AIDS symptoms if you're infected with the AIDS virus.
2. If you're infected with the AIDS virus, there's a better than fifty-fifty chance that you'll pass this along to your baby, before birth, during birth, or possibly through breastfeeding.

***My husband and I would like to have a child and feel there's an outside possibility we might be infected with the AIDS virus. What should we do?***

If you or your husband is at risk for AIDS, or if you think there's the slightest possibility that you may be infected, you should both consider the consequences of having the mother's immune system weakened and of bearing a child infected with AIDS.

You should *both* be tested before you conceive a baby.

| Passing AIDS on to your infant is a serious form of child abuse. |
|---|

Pre-test and post-test counseling will probably be very helpful.

We would hope that couples who are HIV-positive will delay pregnancy until more is known about the transmission of AIDS from mothers to infants.

***I have very recently become pregnant and know that my partner is HIV-positive. Do I have to wait three to six months to get an accurate test result? By then it may be too late to have a safe abortion. Should I have an abortion now to be safe?***

If you think you've contracted the virus in the last three months (that is, recently enough so that your antibodies won't have had time to develop), we would advise that you be tested anyway.

If you test negative, you can have a follow-up test in several months, which will either confirm your fears or set your mind at rest. As part of the testing procedure you will be offered counseling, which may help with the difficult decision you are facing.

Meanwhile, take care of yourself as if you already had the virus:

1. Stop any risky behavior. Even if you are HIV-infected, you can keep being reinfected, making it increasingly possible that you will develop AIDS symptoms. You also run the risk of reinfecting your partner and infecting your unborn baby.

2. Take care of your physical health. Remember, pregnancy increases the chances of your developing symptoms if you have the virus. Get medical and nutritional counseling. Eat as sensibly as you can afford. And get plenty of sleep, fresh air, and exercise.

3. Take care of your attitude. Your emotions affect your immune system and your ability to heal, not to mention the health of your unborn baby. We can advise that you stay stress-free, but your circumstances are already stressful. Do the best you can.

4. Understand your relationship with your infected partner. If this is an otherwise healthy relationship, work out with him some safer-sex guidelines you're both willing to live with. If it's not a healthy relationship, get help in improving it or in removing yourself from it.

5. Only you can make the decision whether to carry your baby to term. Enlist the regular support of a counselor, either privately or through a clinic.

***I'm already two months pregnant, and I just found out that I'm HIV-positive. What do I do?***

You and your partner have to consider your options. You may find it helpful to do this with a professional counselor or therapist. (See how to find and evaluate a counselor in Chapter 9.) You may also want to talk with people who represent your emotional support system: relatives, close friends, your minister, or your doctor.

Basically, you have two options:

1. To continue the pregnancy with the 50 to 60 percent chance that your child will be born with the AIDS virus.

2. To have an abortion. At this stage of your pregnancy, by the way, having an abortion does not represent a significant physical risk for you (at least when weighed against the alternative).

In either case, if you develop symptoms, you could become sick and die. And you must consider the implications of this fact for your baby, along with the implications for yourself.

Whatever your decision, it can be very complex and difficult, and it is one that only you can make. You owe it to yourself, to your unborn child, and to your family to obtain accurate information on which to base your decision.

***What about artificial insemination? Is it safe?***

Insemination without testing is dangerous. In fact, several women in Australia contracted AIDS from artificial insemination by an untested donor.

In 1984, United States sperm banks began routine blood testing for HIV of all prospective donors. Some sperm banks require the donor to have a follow-up HIV-antibody test before they will release the sperm.

If you plan to use a known donor rather than an anonymous one, you can have his sperm frozen at a sperm bank while waiting for his HIV follow-up test.

### *Suppose my baby is born with AIDS?*

Some AIDS babies are born with symptoms, and some are born looking quite healthy. If your baby is born with AIDS, you'll need all the support you can get, not only medical but also counseling and peer support.

Most babies born with the AIDS virus have died by the age of 2. [5]

## *Single, Sexual, and Safe*

This section answers questions specifically for women who are dating or thinking about it. It acknowledges special issues that concern young women and re-entry women, those who are newly dating again after a long-term relationship or after a long period without a relationship.

### *I'm newly separated and re-entering the dating scene. How can I protect myself from getting the AIDS virus?*

Many of the suggestions offered in this book will help you practice safer sex and enjoy safe encounters. Protecting yourself means both physical and emotional protection. Physically, you need to use "safe" and "safer" techniques that prevent blood, semen, and vaginal fluids from entering your body, through your vagina, rectum, or mouth. Chapters 3 to 6 outline in detail how you can have sexual pleasure with relative safety.

Emotional protection involves trusting yourself and your partner before you engage in sexual activities (see Chapters 1 and 2).

Safe sex will involve you and a partner in serious conversations that might not have occurred in a new dating situation before the AIDS epidemic.

You can keep in mind the following guidelines:

1. If you or your partner use IV drugs, get help.
2. Never share needles with anyone, and never use re-bagged needles.

3. There's no such thing as completely safe intercourse with an infected partner, even if you use condoms and spermicide.
4. Make careful choices about the sexual activities you will engage in, and negotiate with your partner for safe or safer sexual practices.
5. Semen, blood (including menstrual blood), and vaginal fluids can spread the AIDS virus during contact with them, so choose sexual activities that prevent these fluids from entering your mouth, vagina or anus.
6. Small amounts of the virus have been found in tears and saliva, but as of this writing, there have been no proven cases of AIDS spread through them.
7. For protection against the virus use condoms (with spermicide containing at least 5 percent nonoxynol-9) and throw the condoms away after each use.
8. Use your own sex toys (such as vibrators and dildos), and clean them after each use with bleach or rubbing alcohol (never use bleach or rubbing alcohol internally).
9. Don't mix alcohol or other drugs with sexual activity. They may cloud your judgment and weaken your immune system.

**REMEMBER** Unsafe, unprotected sex with one partner may be more dangerous than safer sex with several.

***In the past I only had to think about birth control, but lately I've become aware that now it's birth control plus preventing disease. I also have to deal with the fact that I may have been exposed to the AIDS virus years ago. What do I do?***

You're right, you have to continue to use whatever birth-control method feels right and works best for you. Plus you have to use condoms and spermicide in addition to your birth control method.

If you feel you've been at risk for contracting the AIDS virus, you should be tested for the antibodies. The testing comes with counseling.

You'll also have to communicate much more openly with any person with whom you are considering sexual contact. That's a lot to consider when entering a new relationship, but it's also taking responsibility for your own health and life.

***How do I bring up the topic of safer sex with a new partner?***

The clearest way is to be direct. Tell the person that you'd like to get to know him better and that you're concerned about getting AIDS.

Ask how the person feels about safer sex practices and what he has done to protect himself. Then share with that person the methods you've decided upon to protect yourself from the AIDS virus.

***My new partner has just told me that he may be at risk for AIDS and is willing to practice safer sex with me. Now I wonder if he is HIV-positive, and I also wonder what he has done in the past that made him feel that he is at risk. What do I do?***

First of all, we'd suggest you thank him for being responsible enough to tell you. We'd then suggest that he have the test for the AIDS antibody so that he will know if he's infected. Perhaps you could offer to go together so that both of you can be tested.

*Remember that you must both refrain from the exchange of body fluids until you're sure he's free of the AIDS virus.* You might consider using some of the pleasure techniques suggested in Chapter 3.

If and when he wants to tell you about his past experiences, that's up to him, but we'd suggest that you not push him on this issue. Rather, accept that he's being open with you, and tell him you'd feel better knowing for sure whether or not he is HIV-positive. You can then talk about how to avoid AIDS risks in the future.

***Are there steps in addition to safe sex that I can take to help protect myself from getting the AIDS virus?***

You can promote good health and improve your immune system with adequate rest, reduction of stress, good nutrition, and regular exercise. Following the rules of good personal hygiene also helps:

- Give specific attention to bathing before and after having sex.
- Use good oral hygiene, keeping your mouth and teeth well cared for.
- Avoid sharing personal items, especially those that may be contaminated by small amounts of blood, such as razors and toothbrushes.
- Make conscious decisions about your personal behavior.

## *Long-Term Safety*

This section answers questions from women in ongoing partnerships. It addresses the issue of safe and safer sex in monogamous relationships.

***My partner and I have been together for eleven years, and we've maintained a mutually faithful relationship. Do we need to practice safer-sex techniques?***

As long as neither of you has used intravenous drugs, had a blood transfusion, or had sex with another partner, you are safe from HIV whether you're heterosexual, gay, or lesbian. You do not have to use condoms, gloves, dental dams, or spermicides (although you may still want to consider some of the suggestions for enhancing sexual pleasure in earlier chapters of this book, and you may want to practice contraception).

But if either of you has had outside sexual relationships in the last ten years (which is true of many more couples than you would think), or if either of you has used intravenous drugs or had a blood transfusion, then you are both at risk.

None of the heterosexual long-term couples we have interviewed reported using safer-sex techniques. This is quite frightening to us, because we're aware that many of these people have had sexual relationships outside their marriages. Most of these relationships have been kept secret from their partners.

We suggest three things to couples like these:

1. Talk openly with your partner.
2. Use safer-sex practices.
3. Both of you be tested confidentially for the AIDS antibody.

***With the use of condoms and spermicides for safer sex, has the incidence of other STDs decreased?***

According to health officials, there was no decrease in the United States in 1986 in either gonorrhea or syphilis. However, studies of gay men showed that their gonorrhea rate has dropped dramatically. This may mean that gay men are practicing safer-sex techniques, and heterosexuals are not.

***How can heterosexuals be reached?***

Through mass education. One of the most successful AIDS education programs for women in the United States is AWARE, in San Francisco. They offer counseling, testing, and education to individuals and groups.

The major mass-media education efforts are now being directed toward women, as if we have to take the major responsibility for safer sex (look at the condom ads on TV or in magazines). Educational programs directed toward heterosexual men also have to be developed. And more TV ads with men from different ethnic groups are needed, to give the message that it is also their responsibility to practice safer sex.

***I suspect that my husband is bisexual. We have very open communications between us, but I've never been able to ask him about this. What do I do?***

We'd suggest you muster up the courage to talk to him about your concerns. Get a counselor to help you if necessary. It's your business, because it may affect your life.

Meanwhile, until you're sure, practice safer-sex techniques and don't exchange body fluids.

> **REMEMBER** A lot of sexual experience *does not* equal a lot of sexual knowledge.

***My husband of twenty years has stopped having sex with me. I'm not aware of anything in our relationship that could have caused him to behave this way. I'm wondering if he's concerned that he's been at risk for AIDS and is afraid to tell me. What do I do?***

Your problem and concern are not unusual. He may suspect he has a risk he hasn't told you about. He may be distraught and frightened that it's too late.

Above all, he may be sending a strong signal that he wants to talk with you. Be supportive. Let him know that you love him.

And if you can bring up the topic of AIDS, especially the information already presented in this book, it may give him the permission and courage to talk to you about his concerns. You may each want to see a counselor alone or together to help you discuss your feelings in an open, nonjudgmental climate.

***Does a man who has had a vasectomy still need to use condoms to practice safer-sex?***

Yes. A man with a vasectomy still releases seminal fluid, even though he no longer releases sperm. The AIDS virus is found in the seminal fluid, as well as in the sperm.

***My husband and I are both HIV-positive. Do we have to practice safer-sex with each other?***

Absolutely!

There are many different strains of the AIDS virus, and the

AIDS virus keeps changing its structure within the body. Thus, if you have unprotected sex, you or your partner may keep exposing each other to new strains.

***My husband died a couple of years ago. I am only in my early sixties and would like to begin dating again. I know I don't have to worry about birth control, but I have been hearing more and more about AIDS recently. I was brought up to believe that good girls didn't talk about sex. I don't know how to bring this up with a man I might be dating. How do I start to talk about sex and AIDS at my age?***

However difficult it feels, you *must* learn how to talk about AIDS to a partner, for safety's sake.

The AIDS virus does not discriminate among people of different age, color, or nationality. A partner your age may have had at least several sexual partners, which puts him at risk for having contracted the AIDS virus.

How do you start? Some women practice by talking into a mirror. Some find it easier to talk to a prospective partner after they've discussed their concerns with a close friend or even with their children or grandchildren. Your children may have a hard time admitting that their mother is a sexual being, even though they may be sexually active adults themselves. Some women tell us that their adult grandchildren are sometimes more accepting, more knowledgeable, and easier to talk with.

***So what do we do about this epidemic?***

Throughout history, epidemics have challenged society and health professionals. AIDS is the most recent example of a major challenge. Unlike many past epidemics, we know the routes of transmission of HIV, so our prevention efforts can be effective. In this respect, society has an advantage, yet the challenge is still tremendous. We can all do our part to educate ourselves, our partners, our family, and our friends. We can set an example by practicing safe- and safer-sex techniques, and encouraging those we love to do the same.

# CHAPTER 8

## *The Birds, the Bees, and the Condoms: Talking with Your Children about Sex and AIDS*

We include a chapter here on talking with children about sex and AIDS because we feel that many women are as concerned about their children's well-being as they are about their own, and so children become an essential part of their safe encounters.

AIDS is a problem that's not going to go away. Even if we find a vaccine tomorrow, many millions are already infected with the AIDS virus, and young people are increasingly at risk. But children who develop a safe-sex consciousness at an early age are much more likely to grow into adults who can handle the complexities of safe sex, with pleasure.

Whether you're a mother, educator, or health-care worker—whatever your relationship is to the children and young adults in your life—chances are that you passionately wish them to have full information about the dangers of AIDS and how to cope. And chances are, too, that you're not sure how to bring up the subject or how to deal with it gracefully if your children should pop questions at you.

Moreover, you may be unclear as to how to talk about sex with your children, and you know that you can't talk in any complete way about AIDS without talking about sex.

When you remember that most women alive today have received no sensitive and consistent sex education, it's no wonder that they may have a hard time becoming sex educators, beyond pointing out occasional birds and bees. How many women do you know who have crossed their fingers and hoped that the sixth-grade menstruation movie would suffice along with the reproduction lectures in high-school biology classes?

But whether you feel you have the skills or not, the AIDS epidemic is forcing you to assume critical responsibility for the sex education of the children in your care. Let us note here that the media may be your ally, because they're sending out information about AIDS (even if they still send out unclear messages about sex and about women's roles). As a result of TV specials, news, and even advertising, children of all ages may be more aware than you think. AIDS is an almost daily presence in their lives, and the word "condom" is becoming a household word, as witnessed by the following conversation between two kindergarten playmates:

First child: "I found a condom on the patio."

Second child: "What's a patio?"

Being able to identify a condom on the patio is not enough. Children of all ages need, and deserve, to have the fullest possible understanding of both AIDS and their sexuality so that they, too, can develop the voice to say Yes to sexual pleasure and No to sex that's physically or emotionally unsafe.

### *How do little children get AIDS?*

The majority of infected children contract AIDS from their infected mothers, either in the uterus or during the birthing process, and a few may acquire it from breastfeeding.

Some children have contracted AIDS from blood transfusion prior to the screening of all donated blood.

### *How do I talk with my children about AIDS when I can't even mention the word "sex" to them?*

You're right. To be able to talk openly with your children about AIDS, you first have to be able to talk about sex, since sexual intercourse is one of the main ways AIDS is spread.

AIDS is a fatal disease. It's important that you try to overcome your discomfort with talking about sexuality and sexual health and learn to give accurate information. If you can't overcome your discomfort, there's nothing wrong with accepting your discomfort and saying so. Even if you don't, your children will sense it anyway.

If you don't know the answer to a question they ask, say so, and then go find the answer.

When you talk with your children about sex and AIDS, that doesn't mean you're giving them permission to rush out and have sexual relationships. It means you're giving them information, and also sharing your personal values.

Here are four tips:

1. Listen to your children's questions, and answer them specifically, and at face value. Don't try to guess at hidden meanings. (Remember the story about the little kid who got the whole birds-and-bees spiel in response to his question, "Where did I come from?" when all he wanted to know was whether he came from Chicago or Peoria.)
2. Be direct. If you avoid the question or give long, drawn-out lectures, you'll frighten or bore them, so they'll stop asking you questions.
3. Use body language that matches your verbal language.
4. If your children don't ask you questions about sex and AIDS, then you'll have to bring up the topic yourself, with age-appropriate information. A good time to do this might be when sex or AIDS is mentioned on a TV program that you and your children are watching.

***If I warn my children about AIDS, won't I be throwing a wet blanket on something that can be very beautiful and special?***

Your concern alone tells us that you want to find a way to talk about AIDS without confusing the beautiful aspects of sex with the consequences of getting the disease. You can give your children information about health and also reinforce your values about positive sexual behaviors.

Talking to your children calmly, in words they can understand, helps them feel comfortable about their own feelings. Find out what they already know and correct any misinformation.

Also, cuddling your children lets them know in a physical way that you think pleasure is wonderful.

## *Talking with Pre-school Children (Birth to 4 Years)*

***I've read that children aren't sexual until after puberty. Why should I be concerned about the education of my infant and toddler?***

Let's correct a myth here, right off the bat. Children are sexual long before puberty. All individuals are sexual beings from the time they are born until the time they die. Some researchers believe our sex lives begin even before birth.

***So how should I begin their sexuality education?***

You can begin your children's sexuality education by having a positive attitude and creating an environment in which the children feel comfortable playing with their own bodies and eventually asking you questions. If you give verbal and nonverbal messages about how wonderful the body is and how good it can feel, you'll help set the foundation for open and honest discussions as they get older.

For instance, your baby and toddler are learning about their bodies and need to have basic facts of life accepted and talked about in a clear, open, and honest manner. As they learn to talk, they need to learn the correct names for their body parts: face, nose, hands, vagina, clitoris, and penis. Keep it simple. They'll usually ask you for specific information, not for a detailed explanation.

***Can the 3-year-olds in my day-care class understand about AIDS?***

Probably not in an abstract way, but they can start learning about what's safe, which is prime training for safe sex as they grow up. They can differentiate between safe, happy touch, and touching that doesn't feel good. They can understand that they shouldn't let certain people touch their genital areas, just as they can understand that they shouldn't play with matches or cross the street alone.

They can understand all these concepts if you use language that's meaningful to them. Try using characters they're familiar with to help them begin to apply the idea of safe touch to their own lives: You might ask them to show what a puppy does when he wants to be touched, and what he does when he doesn't want to be touched. You can tell children that they can learn to say Yes and No to different kinds of touch, just like puppies, kittens, rabbits, turtles, and on and on.

***I noticed my daughter and her friend playing "Mommy and Daddy" and kissing each other. Is this normal?***

Sex play between small children of the opposite sex, and the same sex, is not only normal but also necessary to development. It's sometimes called "rehearsal play" for adulthood.

If there's any harmful effect, it's usually from adults making children feel ashamed and guilty. Instead of laughing at your daughter or expressing shock and trying to control her behavior, you can use this as an opportunity to talk with her about the kinds of things that feel good to her and the kinds of things that feel bad. This way she'll get the idea that pleasure is fine and delightful, and that it's OK to talk about. And she'll be able to begin making distinctions between pleasure and sex play that's coercive or manipulative.

## *Talking with Young Children (5 to 8 Years)*

***What can you tell a child of this age about AIDS?***

You can tell a child that AIDS is a deadly disease. You can say that it's spread through using drugs that are not prescribed by the doctor and through certain kinds of behavior with a person who has the AIDS infection. You can also explain that diseases can get into the blood through cuts in the body.

Children of this age will hear about AIDS on television and from their friends. Give them answers based on facts.

***My son told me that he was asked to play "blood brother" with another child. Isn't this a way of spreading AIDS?***

It's a good idea to tell him that it's not safe to exchange body fluids with another person. You can describe body fluids in words he can understand.

One kind of body fluid is blood. There are diseases, including AIDS, that can be spread through exchanging blood. You can warn him that for this reason, "blood brother" is not safe to play.

***Could my child get AIDS through a fight at school or during contact on the playground?***

There is no evidence that AIDS is transmitted through bumps and bruises, but the infection can theoretically be transferred through scratches and cuts. External contact with blood is much less likely to spread the AIDS virus than the direct injection of blood into the bloodstream which occurs in blood transfusions or in needle sharing among IV drug users.

***Can my child play with a classmate who has AIDS?***

Casual contact is not dangerous. No identified case of AIDS in the United States is known to have been transmitted from one child to another in the home, at school, or in a play setting. There's not even a suspicion that casual contact can transmit AIDS. Even children sharing food, toys, beds, and playpens have not passed the virus between them. In homes where an adult has AIDS, no child in the family has been known to contract the disease through day-to-day contact, including hugging and kissing.

***What if he gets bitten by the child?***

Although the AIDS virus has been identified in saliva, and it is theoretically possible to transmit it through a bite, there are no known cases of AIDS having been transmitted through a bite.

***When should school sex education and AIDS education begin?***

The surgeon general of the United States says in his 1986 report on AIDS that "education concerning AIDS must start at the lowest grade possible as part of any health and hygiene program."[1]

We believe that this can start with age-appropriate information in nursery school and kindergarten, and continue through every grade of school. Children have a right to learn about sexuality and AIDS just as they have a right to learn mathematics, history, and language skills.

Despite the agreement in our society that parents should be the ones to give their children information about sex, very few parents know how to do this positively and effectively (any more than they know how to teach math, history, and grammar). Thus, schools need to take at least some of the responsibility for AIDS education.

## *Talking with Preteens (9 to 12 Years)*

***My 11- and 12-year olds asked me about AIDS. What should I tell them?***

Children at this age are experiencing many emotional, physical, and social changes. They're interested in their bodies and the changes that are taking place. They're curious about sexual behaviors. Some may begin dating, and some may start experimenting in earnest with their friends. They're ready for some sophisticated information about intimacy, sexuality, and disease prevention.

This age group is still receptive to information from their parents—much more so than a little later, when they become adolescents. It's important that you give them accurate, direct, and explicit information about AIDS, how it's spread and how they can protect themselves. You can give them specific information that could save their lives—and you can do it without offering them permission to experiment inappropriately with their sexuality or with drugs.

You can explain simply that the body's protective barrier, the skin, normally prevents infection from agents like HIV. However, if the barrier is broken by injury or by a needle puncture, fluid containing the virus may enter the body. HIV is easily transferred from one person to another in sexual activities that involve the exchange of body fluids, especially if there are any breaks in the skin.

Children this age need to be told specifically that AIDS is transmitted by penis-vagina contact, penis-anus contact, and exposure to contaminated blood. They need to be told about sexual intercourse, same-sex sexual behavior, oral and anal sex, methods of birth control, and safer-sex techniques.

You can explain that if people are going to have sexual intercourse, and there is even the slightest suspicion that either of them may have been infected (perhaps years before), they should first of all be tested, and should by all means use a condom and a spermicide for protection.

You can say you're not telling them all this necessarily in terms of their own behavior now, but in terms of more adult behavior when they grow up.

You may feel it's appropriate and helpful for preteens to read this book, or at least this chapter, for specific information. But you must be ready and able to discuss their concerns and questions with them. *Giving them a book to read does not take the place of open discussions, person-to-person.*

### *What should I discuss with my preteens about right and wrong?*

You can tell them you know they're getting mixed messages about sexual morality. One message is that it's right to have sex only when you're married. The other message comes from watching television or movies, and that is that: Anything goes.

Emphasize that with AIDS, the issue is not what you think is right or wrong: The issue is the need to protect your life.

Discuss the importance of:

1. Staying away from street drugs and needles
2. Not having sex until you're ready and responsible
3. Not having sex with someone unless you can be positive that person does not have the AIDS virus
4. Being sure when you have intercourse that the man wears a condom and the woman uses a spermicide
5. Not having sex with lots of different people
6. Not having sex with a prostitute
7. Not having anal sex
8. Saying No to *anyone's* pressure to have sexual intercourse

***I'm concerned that our daughter and her boyfriend are experimenting with petting. Is this safe?***

It's normal at this age to be sexually adventurous, with both the opposite sex and the same sex, and it's normal for your daughter and her boyfriend to be kissing and touching each other's bodies, and even each other's genitals.

What's sad is that your daughter and her friend are coming of age sexually at a time when sexual intercourse and perhaps even genital petting hold such dangers. However, this is your chance to help them become used to the necessity for safe and safer sex.

*Becoming comfortable with safe- and safer-sex techniques when they are just beginning to experiment sexually may help young people continue the habit of safety throughout their lives.*

You need to let your daughter know that there are no documented cases of AIDS being transmitted by petting. But, in so-called heavy petting, below the belt, it is possible that seminal fluid or vaginal fluid could enter hangnails or small cuts on the fingers. This is true even if there is no orgasm or ejaculation.

Our suggestion for safe sex would be to recommend that

they stroke and massage each other with their clothes on, not touching each other's bare genitals.

If they absolutely *must* touch each other without clothes, they risk exchanging seminal or vaginal fluids. Then we suggest they wear latex gloves. (Inexpensive, unsterile gloves can be purchased in a drugstore; suggestions for their purchase and use are in Chapter 4.)

Your daughter is likely to act totally mortified at this suggestion and insist that you have rocks in your head for imagining she would agree to anything so ridiculous. But you can stand your ground as you continue to outline for her the responsibilities necessary these days for personal safety.

> AIDS doesn't just happen to you. Your behavior invites AIDS, and your behavior can prevent it.

## *Talking with Adolescents (13 to 19 Years)*

***My 14-year-old just came home from school and asked: "Hey, Mom, what's this AIDS thing?" What do I say?***

You can tell him that it's a terrible disease that can kill him. It can be spread between people when they have sexual intercourse. Sex can be a beautiful and wonderful experience, but having sex with someone who is infected with the AIDS virus is very dangerous.

You can go on to say that there are many ways to have sex that are quite safe because they don't involve the exchange of body fluids. And you can emphasize that it's important to develop a relationship before getting physical with another person.

Because many 14-year-olds are at a stage where they're experimenting with drugs as well as sex, it's also important to talk about how AIDS can be passed from person to person through needles when IV drug users shoot up.

You might want to use strong language here: "IV-drug use is always destructive, but now it's more of a killer than ever."

***My 17-year-old son asked: "How do you know if someone is infected with the AIDS virus?"***

You can let him know that's very difficult to tell. Most people who are infected, and who are therefore *infectious,* don't even know it themselves, so you might not be able to tell for sure by asking them. But anyone can be tested to find out.

***He then went on to ask: "Does this mean nobody can have sex unless they're married?" Now what do I say?***

You can say that it may mean that to some people but that others will have intercourse with one or even several different people before they settle down in marriage. There is certainly some physical risk in that. They'd need to learn about safe-sex and safer-sex techniques, and practice them consistently.

You can say that he can decide how safe from risk of infection he wants to be and that he can determine the behaviors that will keep him that safe. You can remind him that some behaviors that are safe are also very satisfying. These are hugging, kissing, stroking, massaging, holding someone very close, moving bodies against each other with clothes on, lots of talk, laughing, and open discussion.

You can go on to say that these behaviors will keep him absolutely safe, as long as he stays away from IV drugs and shared needles. These behaviors will also give him an opportunity to get to know someone well, to develop trust and a knowledge of the other person's history and lifestyle.

This is also an opportunity for him to practice making careful decisions about important issues in his life, and the kinds of decisions he makes can indicate his care for himself and his partner.

You can warn him that if he finds that he or his partner are putting pressure on each other, or manipulating or scheming, he'll know he's in an unhealthy relationship. People who act like this often don't like themselves very much, and they have difficulty liking anyone else, much less loving them. Make it clear that if someone behaves like this, he'd better be cautious about having a relationship with that person.

***A 13-year-old asks if you can get AIDS from deep, tongue, or French kissing.***

This is a question that has no straight yes or no answer.

There have been no reported cases traced to deep kissing. But the AIDS virus is found to some degree in all body fluids—blood, semen, vaginal secretions, tears, and also saliva. Deep kissing with someone who is HIV-infected might theoretically spread AIDS, but it's much, much less dangerous than unprotected intercourse or sharing needles.

***A 15-year-old girl reports: "Although I have had sex, I've decided I don't want to do it again unless I'm really in love. But I have a problem saying No."***

You can begin by supporting her decision and telling her that it's OK to say No to having sex with someone because you choose not to. Not having sexual intercourse is the surest way to avoid the AIDS virus, and pregnancy, too.

You can then validate her problem by saying how hard it is for women to make their own decisions about sex and stand up for their own feelings. You can reiterate for her that guys won't always listen to her and may try to talk her into having intercourse with them, no matter what she says. They may try to make her feel as if she's being mean or depriving them of their right to pleasure. Or they may call her a prude.

You can encourage her to find more than one way to say No, and even practice conversations with her.

Finally, you can tell her that there are many ways of expressing love that include closeness and pleasurable physical feelings without intercourse. (If you run short of ideas, check Chapters 3 and 6.)

***My 18-year-old daughter asks: "Do condoms really work?"***

Condoms aren't perfect, but they do help.

We suggest your daughter read Chapter 4, which gives a comprehensive outline of why condoms work and why they don't, and also gives guidelines on how to buy them and use them.

It's important for your daughter to understand that condoms aren't the whole story. She should know her partner well before she decides to have intercourse. You can say to her: "*When you have sex with someone, you're having sex with all his previous partners.*"

You can also remind her: "If a guy says No to using condoms, what's he saying about how much he cares about you? Love, caring, respect, and consideration are necessary for a good relationship."

And be sure to make clear to her not to depend on her partner to have the condoms. She should carry condoms with her, and also spermicide containing nonoxynol-9.

### *What about alcohol, pot, coke, and acid?*

This message bears repeating over and over: *Don't have sex when you're drunk or high.* Sex feels great and is its own high. Alcohol and drugs can affect your judgment as well as your immune system.

### *Do adolescents need to be as concerned about the AIDS virus as adults do?*

The risks to adolescents of coming into contact with the AIDS virus is growing, and may be even higher than for adults.

Why is this? First of all, they're experimenting more with sexual behaviors. Many individuals diagnosed in their twenties with AIDS (about 21 percent of the cases reported in 1986) were probably infected during their teens. Statistics show that young people between the ages of 13 and 19 have a very high rate of other STDs (an estimated 2.5 million had STDs in 1987, and the nation's highest rate of gonorrhea is found in women 15 to 19 years old).[2] There's no reason to believe that exposure to the AIDS virus is any less.

Also, many teenagers mix sex and drugs, which can cloud judgment, make for carelessness, and create opportunities for the transmission of AIDS.

***Why is it so hard to communicate about safe sex with adolescents?***

Preventive efforts are complicated by developmental issues. Teenagers are naturally concerned with "Who am I" questions and with self-esteem. Relationships with their peers become all-important. They experiment with greater independence, and many begin to identify moral codes, and test behaviors that are different from those of their parents.

This questioning of parents and other adults is usually healthy, because it allows young people to define their own sense of self. But it can lead to frustration for the educator who hopes to teach the risks of sexual intercourse and IV drug use, along with other hazards such as smoking, and drinking and driving.

***My daughter seems to have the attitude that she can take risks and nothing bad will happen to her. She says she won't be concerned about the dangers of AIDS until someone she knows dies.***

It's normal for young adults to have difficulty imagining a future beyond today. And it's also normal for them to see themselves as invulnerable. The differences between your daughter's perspective and yours make it especially difficult for you to educate her about AIDS.

Her attitudes keep her from comprehending the risks of a lethal disease that has an incubation period of many years, or understanding that she must practice safer-sex techniques and avoid IV drug use or she could die in her twenties. Compare how hard it is to convince this group not to mix drinking and driving, even though many have lost friends in fatal accidents.

***So how can parents and educators reach teenagers?***

One of the most effective ways of reaching teenagers with any information is through peer education groups. They're effective in changing attitudes about AIDS because peers have such a powerful influence on the decisions people this age make about their sex and drug behaviors.

You can help arrange a peer education group in your school or community.

You can also help establish comprehensive family life education programs with well-trained teachers who can facilitate peer groups and question any harmful group norms.

> AIDS-risk activities are not found just in "bad kids" or troubled youths. AIDS-prevention education must be made available to all young adults.

## *Talking with Adults (College-Age and Older)*

Adults college-age and older may need just as much guidance about AIDS and safe sex as children and adolescents. Growing beyond adolescence does not guarantee knowledge—one needs only to look at the statistics.

In one college it was reported that:

> Jane got AIDS from a boyfriend she broke up with four years ago. She didn't know he was bisexual, and he didn't know he was infected with AIDS.
>
> Dave got AIDS from sharing drug needles. He gave it to his girlfriend. Their baby has AIDS, too.
>
> Mike got AIDS from a homosexual experience he'd had when he was 15. He was out of college and starting his first job when he got sick.
>
> Joe caught it from a prostitute.
>
> Linda thinks she got AIDS from a guy she knew in her old high school, but she's not sure.

This list could go on and on.

Jane, Dave, Mike, Joe, and Linda—each of them was contagious unknowingly, and all of them may have given AIDS to any of the other partners they had sexual intercourse with along the way.

### *What are colleges doing to educate students about AIDS?*

Most college health centers have educational programs, some have peer education programs, and some have AIDS awareness weeks. Condoms are often given out free, and counseling is available.

### *Are these programs helping?*

That's hard to tell. This age group is as high a risk group as adolescents, maybe higher. They're more independent from their families and, consequently, more experimental, both with multiple sex partners and with drugs.

Informal studies conducted on college campuses and in bars indicate that students have some awareness of AIDS but that most still feel it can't happen to them. They seem to be in denial and are not practicing safe- or safer-sex techniques.[3]

However, some college students are reporting a high degree of AIDS awareness and peer pressure to use safer-sex techniques. As one 20-year-old put it: "I worry more about my 26-year-old sister than myself, because I've had a lot more education about AIDS. She graduated before the education programs began."

### *What about other STDs in this age group?*

STDs are very prevalent among teens and this age group. For example, the highest rate of chlamydia for both sexes is between the ages of 15 and 24. The highest rate of gonorrhea is in men 20 to 24 years, and genital herpes is highest in women 20 to 24 and men 25 to 29.[4]

In conclusion, even when our children become adults, they need our concern and support in their sexual decision-making and in learning new habits of expressing their sexuality. Educating people to change their behaviors is the only way we know how to prevent AIDS at this time. It's crucial that we be able to communicate openly and freely with all our children about AIDS and sex. But in the zeal to keep our children safe from AIDS, we must take care that we don't teach them to destroy their pleasure in sex.

However you decide to communicate with your children on this vital subject, we urge you to offer sex-positive messages, both verbally and nonverbally—messages like: "I agree that sex is beautiful and that AIDS is frightening. That makes it especially important for you to be responsible and careful and to follow the guidelines suggested for safe sex."

We hope that out of all the fear and concern that is plaguing the world today, a new sexual ethic will develop, an ethic of individual responsibility based on pleasure.

# CHAPTER 9

## *Help—and How to Ask for It*

We recognize that reading this book may not be enough to provide you with all the information and support you need to ensure a vital sex life that is free of disease.

And we recognize that for many women, safe sex goes well beyond preventing AIDS and other STDs. In fact, your sexual encounters may put you in a variety of risk-filled situations. You may have to confront fears and performance difficulties in yourself or your partner. You may find yourself faced with sexual coercion. You may be feeling the fallout from sexual abuse, incest, or rape. Or you may have sought help from a professional only to find that professional sexually exploiting you.

This chapter highlights AIDS resources, mail-order houses for safe-sex equipment, and some other resources that may be appropriate if you're having a problem with sexual dysfunction, unsafe sex, or an unsafe relationship.

Before we list addresses and phone numbers, here's a description of some of the kinds of help that are available and what you can expect from them.

What's the difference between counseling and therapy? Counseling is a short-term (often one-shot) relationship with a trained individual who offers information, suggestions, and support to help you solve a specific problem. Therapy goes beyond the counseling contract. Therapists usually have more comprehensive training than counselors and seek to help you work through your problem, often dealing with primal feelings along the way. Therapy is therefore usually more intensive and long-term than counseling.

## *AIDS Counseling*

Free counseling is often offered as part of the routine of testing for the AIDS antibody. When you're making arrangements to be tested, make sure both pre-test and post-test counseling will be available for you.

### Pre-test Counseling

This is a chance for you to ask questions and express anxieties, and also a chance to make sure your test will be anonymous, or at least confidential.

When you go for your test, a trained counselor will be on hand not only to hear you out but to educate you about the process of the test, what the test determines, what the results may mean, and what steps you should take if you test positive.

Your counselor will explain the "window"—that period of time (three to six months or more) between the moment of infection and the appearance of antibodies to the virus.

In addition, your counselor will advise you to practice safe sex until you know for sure that you're free of the AIDS virus. And your counselor will give you some specific safe-sex guidelines.

### Post-test Counseling

This is where you get your results, which should *always* be conveyed in person, not over the phone.

If your test is *negative*, your counselor may encourage you to repeat the test after a period of time, to make sure you were not tested before antibodies had time to form. In any event, your counselor will encourage you to stay risk-free and will provide you with information on safe and safer sex.

If your test is *positive,* your counselor will help you understand what a positive result means and help you interpret whether it may be a so-called *false positive.*

Your counselor is trained to do the following to evaluate how you are likely to cope with a positive test result:

- Review your situation to make sure you understand what a positive test result could mean for you
- Advise you on how to practice safe sex and safer sex
- Advise you to inform your present and former partners
- Assess your emotional reaction

Shock, grief, and anger are all parts of the normal range of emotion here. But if your counselor suspects that you are in complete denial or that your reaction is psychotic or suicidal, he or she will refer you for intensive therapy to help you cope with your feelings and your situation.

## *Sex Therapy*

Sex therapy is usually a series of sessions focusing on the who-what-why-where-when-how of specific sexual dysfunctions.

The usual aim of sex therapy is to motivate a change in the sexual performances of you and/or your partner, so that in fairly short order you'll be able to enjoy pleasure, intercourse, orgasm, or whatever you present as a goal. A sex therapist should also be able to help you discover techniques for safe sex. A sex therapist may work with you alone or with you and your partner together. If you do not have a partner, a sex therapist may occasionally suggest you work with a partner surrogate, who is trained to teach you new techniques directly, in rehearsal sessions set up like actual sexual encounters with a partner.

How do you pick a sex therapist? You may opt for a single therapist or a team, a Ph.D. or an M.D., a woman or a man, a private practitioner or one who works in a hospital or clinic. Sex therapists come in all shapes and sizes, and they often do something else, like clinical psychology, family therapy, or social work. The discipline of sex therapy came into being because these other disciplines don't train their professionals to deal with sexuality.

If you think you're a candidate for sex therapy and aren't sure where to look for a sex therapist, you can check with the American Association of Sex Educators, Counselors, and Therapists (AASECT), the only accrediting organization in the United States for sex therapists. There are AASECT-certified sex therapists in every state; all have had training and supervision in sex therapy and have agreed to follow a code of professional ethics.

Be aware that sex therapy may lead you into examining other facets of your life and may possibly lead you into other forms of therapy. One of the difficulties with focusing only on sex is that, ideally, sex doesn't exist in isolation from the rest of your life. In fact, your sexual problem may be the tip of an iceberg, the part that shows. As you begin to explore, you may become acutely aware of underlying problems in yourself and your relationship.

## *Psychotherapy*

If you start looking for psychotherapy, you may find that there is a kind to meet almost every need. You can opt for psychoanalysis, where you meet with your analyst several times a week for a number of years; or you can choose briefer, more active and dynamic therapies such as gestalt, psychodrama, behavior modification, psychosynthesis, or even body-oriented therapies such as bioenergetics.

Some women may be glad to hear that there is such a thing as feminist therapy, which sees cultural conditioning as responsible for many of the problems women present as personality disturbances. Feminist therapy attempts to equalize, as much as it can, the power imbalance between therapist and client.

Whichever modality you choose, an important fact to remember is that the quality of therapy you receive most often depends on your own readiness, and on the skills and personality of your therapist.

## Individual Therapy

In this form of therapy you meet on a regular basis, one-on-one with your therapist, with support for identifying your emotional problems and working them through.

## Relationship Therapy

Also called "couples" therapy or "marital" therapy, this is where you and your partner meet with a therapist, or sometimes a team of co-therapists.

The issue here is not the individual, but the relationship and its dynamics, such as how you and your partner communicate your needs and desires to each other.

## Family Therapy

The format can vary, depending on circumstances. Your entire family may meet with one or two therapists or a team of therapists, including school counselor, social worker, physician, and any other relevant person. Or parts of your family may meet, or one person may meet alone with the therapist or therapists.

What differentiates family therapy from all other kinds is

that the client is the whole family system, never just one individual.

## Group Therapy

In this form of therapy, several unrelated clients meet together with one or more trained facilitators. The group may be a general therapy group or may have a special emphasis such as sexuality, sexual abuse, illness, or divorce. Group therapy widens your pool of information, feedback, and validation beyond your therapist, your partner, or your family. The group also provides you with peer pressure and encouragement to change painful habits.

Facilitated therapy groups are a prime arena for practicing new behaviors in a safe place, and can be particularly useful in conjunction with individual therapy.

# *Peer Groups*

A peer group has no leader, and so it cannot technically be called therapy even though its effect may be entirely therapeutic.

A prototype of the peer group is the sewing circle of olden days, where neighborhood women used to get together periodically like an extended family. They produced gorgeous quilts, and they gave each other a forum for talking about what was going on in their lives. Together, they provided regular support they could all count on, an environment where no one was either leader or identified patient.

You can probably find a peer group in your neighborhood, but it probably won't be a quilting party. Peer groups today range from women's support groups to groups dealing with subjects such as sexual abuse, incest, and battering. Call your local women's center to find out what's going on.

More and more peer groups are forming in response to various addictions. These are often drop-in groups, and most have twelve-step formats dictated by national headquarters: AA (Alcoholics Anonymous), NA (Narcotics Anonymous), Al-Anon (for families and friends of substance abusers), ACOA (Adult Children of Alcoholics), and SA (Sexaholics Anonymous), to mention a few.

The AIDS epidemic is spawning its own support groups, both for AIDS prevention and for people with AIDS and their families and friends.

## *What Is Safe Therapy?*

Safe therapy leaves you feeling better, not worse, just as safe sex gives you pleasure, not abuse or disease.

What should you be able to expect from therapy?

Reasonable, baseline expectations are that a therapist provide confidentiality, attention to the problem at hand, familiarity with the problem, and specific skills in dealing with it. Furthermore, you should be able to expect that your therapist will periodically assess your goals and progress with you and that you will mutually decide when you are ready to end the therapy.

If you expect that any therapist will provide a psychic pill you can pop for an overnight cure, that's an unreasonable expectation, and you're bound to be disappointed. Therapy is work, and it's *your* work. Your therapist is only a guide (albeit a trained one) and a human being.

In addition, it's reasonable to have a high degree of confidence that your therapist is acting in your best interests. This trust may spring from appreciation of your therapist's expertise, or it may be more a matter of personal chemistry between you and the therapist. It may even spring from the nature of the relationship; a therapist *ought* to be trustworthy. In any event, the therapeutic relationship is often special and may feel like the most trusting one you ever had.

Here's a sad paradox of therapy: While this kind of trust can help you climb mountains in terms of your own fears and insecurities, it can also open you up to exploitation.

Most therapists are highly ethical. But we want to issue a warning that some are not; they break the contract of therapy and enter into seductive and sexual relationships with their clients. This is unsafe therapy, not because sex is bad but because the point of therapy is to make clients' lives saner and less painful. Sex between therapists and clients usually accomplishes just the opposite. It emphasizes an already unequal power balance, and becomes a dominance-submission game that undermines the therapy, along with other aspects of a client's life. And, by the way, if therapists are doing their job, it's impossible for them to be seduced by clients, and don't let anyone tell you otherwise.

Sex with your therapist is *not* sex therapy.

## *Red-Flag List*

Here are nine danger signals to alert you that this is the moment to stop being open and trusting, and to check out your therapist's motives. Unless you can be satisfied that you're reading the signals wrong, it may be time for you to end this relationship and find somebody else as a health-care provider.

If your therapist or other health professional does any of the following, he or she is not totally focused on your therapy:

1. Initiates a personal relationship with you while you're still in treatment. This includes inviting you to join in social occasions and professional or business ventures.
2. Asks you to call, except when you are in crisis
3. Makes remarks that put you down, including sexist or racist remarks

4. Breaks confidentiality
5. Makes sexual advances toward you
6. Responds sexually to your sexual advances
7. Tries to convince you that a sexual relationship between the two of you would be good for you
8. Won't agree to your ending treatment, and won't give you a reasonable explanation
9. Wants you to end treatment before you feel ready, and won't give you a reasonable explanation

What do you do if your therapist or other health professional makes sexual advances to you, either physical or verbal? Or tells you that having sex with you is the only way to help you with your problem, including your sexual problem?

1. **Say No**—no matter how tempting the offer is.
2. **Forget your good-girl training, and tell**. And tell your doctor or therapist you're reporting him or her to the state licensing board.
3. **Talk to somebody supportive**—a friend, another therapist, a women's center, or rape-crisis center. Immediately get validation for your point of view. Don't wait.
4. **Get out of treatment with that person.**

## *Where to Find Help*

The following phone numbers and addresses are available to provide specific help. If you send for pamphlets, payment is not required, but a donation of at least $1.00 plus a stamped, self-addressed business envelope would be helpful for the nonprofit AIDS-education organizations. A larger donation is always appreciated.

# *AIDS Hotlines*

The following list of hotline numbers will help you find the latest information available about AIDS, STDs, medications for AIDS, and testing for the HIV antibody.

AZT Hotline at the National Institutes of Health
800-843-9388

National AIDS Hotline
800-342-7514

National Gay Task Force AIDS Crisis
800-221-7044 (5 PM to 10 PM)
212-807-6016 (New York State)

National STD Hotline
800-227-8922

Public Health Service Hotline
800-342-AIDS

You can also call your state department of health for your local AIDS hotline number.

# *AIDS Education and Support Groups*

The following are offered so that you can contact any specific group that might meet your individual needs for information or support.

The names of organizations and individuals listed below were the latest available at the time of printing.

AIDS Action Council
729 Eighth Street, S.E., Suite 200
Washington, DC 20003
202-547-3101

AIDS Action Foundation
729 Eighth Street, S.E., Suite 200
Washington, DC 20003
202-547-3101

American Association of Physicians for Human Rights
P.O. Box 14366
San Francisco, CA 94114
415-558-9353

Gay Men's Health Crisis
Box 274
132 West 24th Street
New York, NY 10011
212-807-6655
212-807-7035

Hispanic AIDS Forum
c/o APRED
853 Broadway, Suite 2007
New York, NY 10003
212-870-1902
212-870-1864

Minnesota AIDS Project
2025 Nicollet Avenue S., Suite 200
Minneapolis, MN 55404
612-870-7773
800-752-4281 (hotline)

Minority Task Force on AIDS
c/o New York City Council of Churches
475 Riverside Drive, Room 456
New York, NY 10115
212-749-1214

National AIDS Information Clearing House of Centers for Disease Control
P.O. Box 6003
Rockville, MD 20850
800-342-2437
800-342-7514

National AIDS Network
1012 14th Street, N.W. Suite 601
Washington, DC 20005
202-347-0390

National Coalition of Gay Sexually Transmitted Disease Services
P.O. Box 239
Milwaukee, WI 53201
414-277-7671

National Council of Churches
AIDS Task Force
475 Riverside Drive, Room 572
New York, NY 10115
212-870-2421

San Francisco AIDS Foundation

Mailing Address:
P.O. Box 6182
San Francisco, CA 94101-6182

Office Addresses:
333 Valencia Street, 4th floor
San Francisco, CA 94103
415-864-4376

[or]

25 Van Ness Avenue, 6th floor
San Francisco, CA 94102
415-864-5855

Hotlines:
800-FOR-AIDS (Northern California)
415-863-AIDS (San Francisco)

Society for the Scientific Study of Sex
AIDS Task Force
P.O. Box 208
Mount Vernon, IA 52314
(Resources for professionals and media only)

U.S. Public Health Service
Public Affairs Office
Hubert H. Humphrey Building, Room 725-H
200 Independence Avenue, S.W.
Washington, DC 20201
202-245-6867

# AIDS Resources for Women

The following groups address specific concerns of women:

AIDS Action Committee
661 Boylston Street
Boston, MA 02116
617-437-6200, ext. 216 (Women's Education)
617-536-7733 (AIDS Action Line)
800-235-2331 (Massachusetts only)

AWARE
San Francisco General Hospital
995 Potrero Avenue
San Francisco, CA 94110
415-476-4091

Gay and Lesbian Counseling Services
6 Hamilton Place
Boston, MA 02108
617-542-5188

Mothers of AIDS Patients (MAP)
P.O. Box 3132
San Diego, CA 92103
619-293-3985

San Francisco AIDS Foundation
Women's Education Program
333 Valencia Street
San Francisco, CA 94103
415-864-4396 (business line)
415-863-AIDS (hotline)

Women's AIDS Project
8235 Santa Monica Boulevard, Suite 201
West Hollywood, CA 90046
213-650-1508

Women and AIDS Counseling Group
Stuyvesant Polyclinic
137 Second Avenue
New York, NY 10003
212-674-0220

Women and AIDS Project
1209 Decater Street, N.W.
Washington, DC 20011

# Where You Can Send for Source Material on AIDS

AIDS
1555 Wilson Boulevard, Suite 700
Rosslyn, VA 22209

AIDS Project of Los Angeles
3570 Wilshire Boulevard, Suite 300
Los Angeles, CA 90010
Office: 213-738-8200
Hotline numbers: 213-876-AIDS
800-922-AIDS (Southern California only)
800-222-SIDA (Southern California, Spanish)

Sex Information and Education Council of the U.S. (SIECUS)
32 Washington Place
New York, NY 10003

Surgeon General's Report on AIDS
National AIDS Information Clearing House of Centers for Disease Control
P.O. Box 6003
Rockville, MD 20850
800-342-7514

# *Materials Specifically for Women*

*AIDS and Safer Sex for Women*
Fenway Community Health Center
16 Haviland Street
Boston, MA 02115

*Lesbians and AIDS*
Women's AIDS Network
333 Valencia Street
San Francisco, CA 94103
415-864-4376

*What Women Should Know about AIDS*
Network Publications
P.O. Box 1830
Santa Cruz, CA 95061-1830

*Women Address AIDS*
Women's AIDS Project
8235 Santa Monica Boulevard
West Hollywood, CA 90046
213-650-1508

*Women Need to Know about AIDS*
Gay Men's Health Crisis, Inc.
Publications Orders
Box 274, 132 West 24th Street
New York, NY 10011
212-807-7517

# *Condom Manufacturers and Distributors*

As we mentioned in Chapter 4, condoms can be purchased by mail. The following is a list of some condom manufacturers and distributors. (We are not endorsing any of the brands of condoms, and we cannot guarantee manufacturer quality.)

A & R Creative Marketing
P.O. Box 110516
Royal Palm Beach, FL 33411

Ansell Americas
78 Apple Street
Tinton Falls, NJ 07724

Barnetts, Inc.
3630 Tryclan Drive
Charlotte, NC 28210

Carter-Wallace
767 Fifth Avenue
New York, NY 10022

Circle Rubber Corporation
408 Frelinghuysen Avenue
Newark, NJ 07114

Mentor Corporation
1499 West River Road North
Minneapolis, MN 55411

National Sanitary Labs
7150 N. Ridgeway
Lincolnwood, IL 60645

Schmid
Rural Route 46W
Little Falls, NJ 07424

Stamford Hygienic Corporation
P.O. Box 932
Stamford, CT 06904

## *Mail-Order Houses Specializing in Books, Vibrators, and Erotic Toys for Women*

Eve's Garden
119 West 57th Street
Suite 1406
New York, NY 10019
212-757-8651
Catalog $1.00

Good Vibrations
3492 22nd Street
San Francisco, CA 94110
415-550-7399
Catalog $1.00

## *Other Resources*

Safe sex is more than AIDS prevention. Here are resources for dealing with rape, incest, sexual abuse, and alcohol and drug abuse. National numbers are listed where available; you will be able to find many of these organizations in your local phone book.

Alcoholics Anonymous World Service, Inc. (AA)
458 Park Avenue South
New York, NY 10016
212-548-1100
(Or call your local AA number)

Al-Anon/Alateen Family Group Headquarters, Inc.
P.O. Box 182
Madison Square Station
New York, NY 10010
212-254-7230
(Or call your local Al-Anon number)

Drug Abuse Treatment
800-662-HELP

Narcotics Anonymous (NA)
800-992-0401

National Association for Children of Alcoholics
13706 Coast Highway, Suite 201
South Laguna, CA 92677-3044
714-499-3889

National Child Abuse Hotline
800-422-4453

Project Inform—Drug Treatment Hotline
800-822-7422
800-334-7422 (California State)

Sexaholics Anonymous (SA)
P.O. Box 300
Simi Valley, CA 93062
805-581-3343

S-Anon (for partners of sexaholics)
P.O. Box 5117
Sherman Oaks, CA 91413
818-990-6910

Women Against Rape (WAR)
(Call your local number or your local rape crisis center)

## *To Find a Therapist*

American Association for Marriage and Family Therapy (AAMFT)
1717 K Street, N.W., Suite 407
Washington, DC 20006
202-429-1825 (A therapist answers your call)

American Association of Sex Educators, Counselors, and Therapists (AASECT)
Eleven Dupont Circle, N.W., Suite 220
Washington, DC 20036
202-462-1171

Association for Women in Psychology (AWP)
P.O. Box 242
Brighton, MA 02135

# Notes and Suggested Readings

## Chapter 1. Safe Sex Begins with You

**NOTES**

1 Forward, S., and Buck, S. (1978) *Betrayal of Innocence.* Harmondsworth, England: Penguin.

**SUGGESTED READINGS**

Belenky M., et al. (1986) *Women's Ways of Knowing: The Development of Self, Voice and Mind.* New York: Basic Books.

Boston Women's Health Collective (1984) *The New Our Bodies, Ourselves.* New York: Simon & Schuster.

French, M. (1979) *The Women's Room.* New York: Doubleday & Co., Inc.

Gilligan, C. (1982) *In a Different Voice: Psychological Theory on Women's Development.* Cambridge, MA: Harvard University Press.

## Chapter 2. The Right Relationship Is a Safe Relationship

**SUGGESTED READINGS**

Forward. S. (1986) *Men Who Hate Women and the Women Who Love Them.* New York: Bantam.

Norwood, R. (1985) *Women Who Love Too Much.* New York: Pocket Books.

Scarf, M. (1986) *Intimate Partners: Patterns in Love and Marriage.* New York: Random House.

Tennov, D. (1979) *Love and Limerence: The Experience of Being in Love.* Briarcliff Manor, NY: Stein & Day.

## Chapter 3. Safe Sex Turns Women On

**NOTES**

1 Ogden, G. (1981) *Perception of Touch in Easily Orgasmic Women during Peak Sexual Experiences.* Unpublished doctoral dissertation. Institute for Advanced Study of Human Sexuality: San Francisco.

2 Califia, P. (1980) *Sapphistry: The Book of Lesbian Sexuality*. Tallahassee, FL: Naiad Press.

3 Pearlman, Patricia, S.H.A.R.E. P.O. Box 188, Palisades Park, NJ 07560.

4 Kerr, C. (1977) *Sex for Women Who Want to Have Fun and Loving Relationships with Equals*. New York: Grove Press.

**SUGGESTED READINGS**

Greene, G. (1986) *Delicious Sex*. New York: Prentice-Hall.

Hite, S. (1976) *The Hite Report: A Nationwide Study of Female Sexuality*. New York: Macmillan.

Loulan, J. (1984) *Lesbian Sex*. San Francisco: Spinsters, Ink.

Stubbs, K.R. and Saulnier, L.A. (1988) *Romantic Interludes, A Sensuous Lovers Guide*. Larkspur, CA: Secret Garden.

## *Chapter 4. The Latex Factor*

**NOTES**

1 Adams, R., Fliegelman, E., and Grieco, A. (1987) Patient guide: How to use a condom. *Medical Aspects of Human Sexuality, 21*, 74–75.

2 Grieco, A. (1987) Cutting the risks for STDs. *Medical Aspects of Human Sexuality, 21*, 70–84.

3 Parachini, A. (1987, August 19) Condoms questioned as a safe way to prevent AIDS, herpes and hepatitis B. *Berkshire Eagle*. p. A8.

4 Conant, M., et al. (1986) Condoms prevent passage of AIDS-associated retrovirus. *Journal of the American Medical Association, 255*, 1706.

5 Adapted from Grieco, A. (1987) Cutting the risks for STDs. *Medical Aspects of Human Sexuality, 21*, 70–84.

**SUGGESTED READINGS**

Everett, J., and Glanze, W.D. (1987) *The Condom Book: the Essential Guide for Men and Women*. New York: New American Library.

Ladas, A. K., Whipple, B., and Perry, J. D. (1982) *The G Spot and Other Recent Discoveries about Human Sexuality*. New York: Holt, Rinehart and Winston.

McIlvenna, T. (ed.) (1987) *The Complete Guide to Safe Sex*. Beverly Hills, CA: Specific Press.

## *Chapter 5. What about Flying Solo?*

**NOTES**

1 Kinsey, A.C., et al. (1953) *Sexual Behavior in the Human Female*. Philadelphia: W.B. Saunders Co.

2 Sandler, J., Myerson, M., and Kinder, B.N. (1980) *Human Sexuality: Current Perspectives*. Tampa, FL: Mariner Publishing Co., Inc.

3 Hite, S. (1976) *The Hite Report*. New York: Macmillan.

4 Sacred Congregation for the Doctrine of the Faith. (1975) *Declaration on Certain Questions Concerning Sexual Ethics*. Rome: Sacred Congregation for the Doctrine of the Faith.

5 Szasz, T. (1970) *The Manufacture of Madness*. New York: Harper & Row.

6 Masson, J.M. (1984) *The Assault on Truth: Freud's Suppression of the Seduction Theory*. New York: Farrar, Strauss & Giroux.

7 Greenback, R. (1961) Are medical students learning psychiatry? *Pennsylvania Medical Journal, 64*, 989–992.

8 Hite, S. (1976) *The Hite Report*. New York: Macmillan.

9 Adapted from Allgeier, E.R., and Allgeier, A.R. (1984) *Sexual Interactions*. Lexington, MA: D.C. Heath and Co.

10 Masters, W.H., and Johnson, V.E. (1966) *Human Sexual Response*. Boston: Little, Brown.

11 Haeberle, E.J. (1978) *The Sex Atlas*. New York: The Seabury Press.

12 Ogden, G. (1981) *Perception of Touch in Easily Orgasmic Women during Peak Sexual Experiences*. Unpublished doctoral dissertation. Institute for Advanced Study of Human Sexuality: San Francisco.

13 Hunt, M. (1974) *Sexual Behavior in the 1970's*. Chicago: Playboy Press.

14 Ladas, A.K., Whipple, B., and Perry, J.D. (1982) *The G Spot and Other Recent Discoveries about Human Sexuality*. New York: Holt, Rinehart & Winston.

**SUGGESTED READINGS**

Barbach, L.G. (1976) *For Yourself: The Fulfillment of Female Sexuality*. New York: Anchor/Doubleday.

Dodson, B. (1987) *Sex for One: The Joy of Selfloving*. New York: Crown.

Friday, N. (1973) *My Secret Garden: Women's Sexual Fantasies*. New York: Pocket Books.

Friday, N. (1975) *Forbidden Flowers: More Women's Sexual Fantasies*. New York: Pocket Books.

## *Chapter 6. Teaching Your Partner to Play*

**SUGGESTED READINGS**

Barbach, L. (ed.) (1984) *Pleasures: Women Write Erotica*. New York: Doubleday.

Barbach, L. (ed.) (1986) *Erotic Interludes: Tales Told by Women*. New York: Doubleday.

Kensington Ladies' Erotica Society. (1984) *Ladies' Own Erotica*. Berkeley, CA: Ten Speed Press.

Kensington Ladies' Erotica Society. (1986) *Look Homeward, Erotica*. Berkeley, CA: Ten Speed Press.

## *Chapter 7. Answers to Questions about AIDS and Other STDs*


**NOTES**

1 Slim, J. (1987) Highlights–Third International Conference on AIDS. *Medical Aspects of Human Sexuality, 21,* 8-13.

2 Finkbeiner, A., Hancock, E., and Schneider, S. (1986) AIDS from specialists at Johns Hopkins. *Johns Hopkins Magazine.* 15-27.

3 Byron, P. (1986) *Women Need to Know about AIDS.* New York: Gay Men's Health Crisis, Inc.

4 VanGelder, L. (1987) AIDS. *MS.* April, 64–71.

5 *Women Address AIDS.* (1986) West Hollywood, CA: The Women's AIDS Project.

**SUGGESTED READINGS**

Kaplan, H.S. (1987) *Women and AIDS.* New York: Simon & Schuster.

Norwood, C. (1987) *Advice for Life: A Woman's Guide to AIDS Risks and Prevention.* New York: Pantheon.

Richardson, D. (1987) *Women and AIDS.* New York: Methuen/Pandora.

Shilts, R. (1987) *And the Band Played On: Politics, People, and the AIDS Epidemic.* New York: St. Martin's Press.


## *Chapter 8. The Birds, the Bees, and the Condoms*


**NOTES**

1 Koop, C.E. (1986) *Surgeon General's Report on Acquired Immune Deficiency Syndrome.* U.S. Department of Health and Human Services.

2 Klein, J. (1987) Scared sexless over AIDS: Advice for the worried well. *American Health.* 83–93.

3 Caron, S.L., Bertram, R.M. and McMullen, T. (1987) AIDS and the college student: The need for sex education. *SIECUS Report, 15,* 6–7.

4 Klein, J. (1987) Scared sexless over AIDS: Advice for the worried well. *American Health.* p. 91.

**SUGGESTED READINGS**

Bell, R., et al. (1987) *Changing Bodies, Changing Lives, rev. ed.* New York: Random House.

Moglia, R., and Welbourne-Moglia, A. (1986) *How to Talk to Your Children about AIDS.* New York: SIECUS.

# Bibliography

Adams, R., Fliegelman, E., and Grieco, A. (1987) Patient Guide: How to use a condom. *Medical Aspects of Human Sexuality*, 21, 74–75.

Allgeier, E. R., and Allgeier, A. R. (1984) *Sexual Interactions*. Lexington, MA: D.C. Heath and Co.

*AIDS and Children*. (1986) U.S. Public Health Service.

Barbach, L.G. (1976) *For Yourself: The Fulfillment of Female Sexuality*. New York: Anchor/Doubleday.

Barbach, L. (ed.) (1986) *Erotic Interludes: Tales Told by Women*. New York: Doubleday.

Barbach, L. (ed.) (1984) *Pleasures: Women Write Erotica*. New York: Doubleday.

Barbach, L., and Levine, L. (1981) *Shared Intimacies: Women's Sexual Experiences*. New York: Bantam Books.

Belenky M., et al. (1986) *Women's Ways of Knowing: The Development of Self, Voice and Mind*. New York: Basic Books.

Bell, R., et al. (1987) *Changing Bodies, Changing Lives, rev. ed.* New York: Random House.

Black, D. (1986) *The Plague Years: A Chronicle of AIDS, the Epidemic of Our Times*. New York: Simon & Schuster.

Blank, J., and Cottrell, H.L. (1978) *I Am My Lover*. Burlingame, CA: Down There Press.

Boston Women's Health Collective. (1984) *The New Our Bodies, Ourselves*. New York: Simon & Schuster.

Brenton, M. (1987) What every woman must know about condoms. *Cosmopolitan*, May, 108–118.

Byron, P. (1986) *Women Need to Know about AIDS*. New York: Gay Men's Health Crisis, Inc.

Calderone, M.S., and Ramey, J.W. (1982) *Talking with Your Child about Sex*. New York: Random House.

Califia, P. (1980) *Sapphistry: The Book of Lesbian Sexuality*. Tallahassee, FL: Naiad Press.

Campbell, J.M. (1986) Sexual guidelines for persons with AIDS and at risk for AIDS. *Medical Aspects of Human Sexuality, 20,* 100–103.

Caron, S.L., Bertram, R.M. and McMullen, T. (1987) AIDS and the college student: The need for sex education. *SIECUS Report, 15,* 6–7.

Conant, M. et al. (1986) Condoms prevent passage of AIDS-associated retrovirus. *Journal of the American Medical Association, 255,* 1706.

Corinne, T., and Lapidus, J. (1982) *Yantras of Womanlove.* Tallahassee, FL: Naiad Press.

Corman, L.C. (1985) The relationship between nutrition, infection, and immunity. *Medical Clinics of North America, 69,* 3.

Dodson, B. (1974) *Liberating Masturbation.* New York: Bodysex Designs.

Dodson, B. (1987) *Sex for One: The Joy of Selfloving.* New York: Crown.

Everett, J., and Glanze, W.D. (1987) *The Condom Book: The Essential Guide for Men and Women.* New York: New American Library.

Finkbeiner, A., Hancock, E., and Schneider, S. (1986) AIDS from specialists at Johns Hopkins. *Johns Hopkins Magazine.* 15–27.

Forward, S. (1986) *Men Who Hate Women and the Women Who Love Them.* New York: Bantam.

Forward, S., and Buck, S. (1978) *Betrayal of Innocence.* Harmondsworth, England: Penguin.

Frazier, G., and Frazier, B. (1973) *The Bath Book.* San Francisco: Troubador Press.

French, M. (1979) *The Women's Room.* New York: Doubleday.

Friday, N. (1975) *Forbidden Flowers: More Women's Sexual Fantasies.* New York: Pocket Books.

Friday, N. (1973) *My Secret Garden: Women's Sexual Fantasies.* New York: Pocket Books.

Gilligan, C. (1982) *In a Different Voice: Psychological Theory on Women's Development.* Cambridge, MA: Harvard University Press.

Graber, B., and Kline-Graber, G. (1979) Female orgasm: Role of pubococcygeus muscle. *Journal of Clinical Psychiatry, 40,* 34–39.

Greenback, R. (1961) Are medical students learning psychiatry? *Pennsylvania Medical Journal, 64,* 989–992.

Greene, G. (1986) *Delicious Sex.* New York: Prentice-Hall.

Greenspan, M. (1983) *A New Approach to Women and Therapy: How Psychotherapy Fails Women and What They Can Do about It.* New York: McGraw-Hill.

Grieco, A. (1987) Cutting the risks for STDs. *Medical Aspects of Human Sexuality, 21,* 70–84.

Guinan, M.E., and Hardy, A. (1987) Epidemiology of AIDS in Women in the United States, 1981–1986. *Journal of the American Medical Association, 257,* 2039–2042.

Haeberle, E.J. (1978) *The Sex Atlas.* New York: The Seabury Press.

Harris, C., Small, C.B. and Klein, R.S. (1983) Immunodeficiency in female sexual partners of men with AIDS. *New England Journal of Medicine, 308,* 1181–1184.

Helmering, D. W. (1986) *Happily Ever After: Why Men and Women Think Differently*. New York: Warner Books.

Hite, S. (1976) *The Hite Report: A Nationwide Study of Female Sexuality*. New York: Macmillan.

Hunt, M. (1974) *Sexual Behavior in the 1970's*. Chicago: Playboy Press.

Hyde, M.O., and Forsyth, E.H. (1987) *Know about AIDS*. Walker and Co.

Kaplan, H.S. (1987) *Women and AIDS*. New York: Simon & Schuster.

Kensington Ladies' Erotica Society (1984) *Ladies' Own Erotica*. Berkeley, CA: Ten Speed Press.

Kensington Ladies' Erotica Society (1986) *Look Homeward, Erotica*. Berkeley, CA: Ten Speed Press.

Kerr, C. (1977) *Sex for Women Who Want to Have Fun and Loving Relationships with Equals*. New York: Grove Press.

Kinsey, A.C., et al. (1953) *Sexual Behavior in the Human Female*. Philadelphia: W.B. Saunders Co.

Klein, J. (1987) Scared sexless over AIDS: Advice for the worried well. *American Health*. 83–93.

Koop, C.E. (1986) *Surgeon General's Report on Acquired Immune Deficiency Syndrome*. Washington, D.C.: U.S. Public Health Service.

Kubler-Ross, E. (1987) *AIDS: The Ultimate Challenge*. New York: Macmillan.

Kushi, M., and Cottrell, M. (1987) *AIDS: Cause and Solution: The Macrobiotic Approach to Natural Immunity*. Boston: Kodansha.

Ladas, A.K., Whipple, B., and Perry, J.D. (1982) *The G Spot and Other Recent Discoveries about Human Sexuality*. New York: Holt, Rinehart and Winston.

Loulan, J. (1984) *Lesbian Sex*. San Francisco: Spinsters, Ink.

Magallon, D.T. (1987) Counseling patients with HIV infections. *Medical Aspects of Human Sexuality*, *21*, 6, 129–147.

Marmor, M., et al. (1986) Possible female-to-female transmission of human immunodeficiency virus. *Annals of Internal Medicine*, *105*, 969.

Masson, J.M. (1984) *The Assault on Truth: Freud's Suppression of the Seduction Theory*. New York: Farrar, Straus & Giroux.

Masters, W.H., and Johnson, V.E. (1966) *Human Sexual Response*. Boston: Little, Brown and Co.

Masters, W. H., Johnson, V. E., and Kolodny, R. C., (1988) *Crisis: Heterosexual Behavior in the Age of AIDS*. New York: Grove Press.

Maugh, T.H. (1987) 27 new drugs to stop AIDS. *American Health*, *6*, 73–84.

McIlvenna, T. (ed.) (1987) *The Complete Guide to Safe Sex*. Beverly Hills, CA: Specific Press.

Miller, J.B. (1976) *Toward A New Psychology of Women*. Boston: Beacon Press.

Moglia, R., and Welbourne-Moglia, A. (1986) *How to Talk to Your Children about AIDS*. New York: SIECUS.

Morgan, R. (1982) *The Anatomy of Freedom*. New York: Anchor Press/Doubleday.

Nomadic Sisters, The (1976) *Loving Women*. Sonora, CA: Authors.

Norwood, C. (1987) *Advice for Life: A Woman's Guide to AIDS Risks and Prevention*. New York: Pantheon.

Norwood, R. (1985) *Women Who Love Too Much*. New York: Pocket Books.

Pearsall, P. (1987) *Superimmunity*. New York: McGraw-Hill.

Pekkanen, J. (1987) AIDS: The plague that knows no boundaries. *Reader's Digest*. June, 49–58.

Perry, J.D., and Whipple, B. (1981) Pelvic muscle strength of female ejaculators: Evidence in support of a new theory of orgasm. *The Journal of Sex Research, 17*, 22–39.

Prudden, B. (1978) *Exer-sex*. Stockbridge, MA: Aquarian Press.

Quackenbush, M. (1987) Educating youth about AIDS. *FOCUS: A Review of AIDS Research, 2*, 1–3.

Richardson, D. (1987) *Women and AIDS*. New York: Methuen/Pandora.

Sandler, J. et al. (1980) *Human Sexuality: Current Perspectives*. Tampa, FL. Mariner Publishing Co., Inc.

Scarf, M. (1986) *Intimate Partners: Patterns in Love and Marriage*. New York: Random House.

Scarf, M. (1980) *Unfinished Business: Pressure Points in the Lives of Women*. New York: Doubleday and Co., Inc.

Shilts, R. (1987) *And the Band Played On: Politics, People, and the AIDS Epidemic*. New York: St. Martin's Press.

Slim, J. (1987) Highlights—Third International Conference on AIDS. *Medical Aspects of Human Sexuality, 21*, 8–13.

Starhawk. (1979) *The Spiral Dance: A Rebirth of the Ancient Religion of the Great Goddess*. New York: Harper & Row.

Steinem, G. (1983) *Outrageous Acts and Everyday Rebellions*. New York: Holt, Rinehart and Winston.

Stubbs, K.R., and Saulnier, L.A. (1988) *Romantic Interludes, A Sensuous Lovers Guide*. Larkspur, CA: Secret Garden.

Szasz, T. (1970) *The Manufacture of Madness*. New York: Harper and Row.

Tavris, C., and Sadd, S. (1977) *The Redbook Report on Female Sexuality: 100,000 Married Women Disclose the Good News about Sex*. New York: Delacort.

*Teens and AIDS: Playing It Safe*. (1987) American Council of Life Insurance and Health Insurance Association of America.

Tennov, D. (1979) *Love and Limerence: The Experience of Being in Love*. Briarcliff Manor, NY: Stein & Day.

VanGelder, L. (1987) AIDS. *MS*. April, 64–71.

Viorst, J. (1986) *Necessary Losses: The Loves, Illusions, Dependencies and Impossible Expectations That All of Us Have to Give Up in Order to Grow*. New York: Simon & Schuster.

Volberding, P., and Rhame, F. (1987) *Acquired Immune Deficiency Syndrome*. Minneapolis, MN: Health EduTech, Inc.

*Women Address AIDS*. (1986) West Hollywood, CA: The Women's AIDS Project.

Wofsy, C.B. (1987) Human immunodeficiency virus infection in women. *Journal of the American Medical Association, 257*, 2074–2076.

Wofsy, C.B., et al., (1986) Isolation of AIDS-associated retrovirus from genital secretions of women with antibodies to the virus. *The Lancet*, 527–529.

# Index

Abortion, 25, 166–167
Abstinence, xvii
Abuse, sexual, 138
  memory of, 46
Abusive relationship, 28–29
Acquired immunodeficiency syndrome (AIDS), 147–175
  abortion and, 166–167
  counseling and, 194–196
  definition of, xvii, 147–150
  denial of, 37–38, 189, 191
  education and support groups and, 202–205
  fear of, 3–4
  hotlines, 202
  long-term relationship and, 25–29, 172–175
  main facts about, 147–155
  pregnancy and, 166–169
  protection of partner and, 27, 36–37, 164
  teaching adults about, 190–192
  teaching children about, 176–190
    adolescents, 185–190
    age 4–8 years, 180–182
    preschool age, 179–180
    preteens, 182–185
  testing for, 3–4, 20, 24, 27, 155–158
  vaccine for, 151
  virus of (see Human immunodeficiency virus (HIV))
  women and, xi–xii, 26, 161–165, 169–172
Ad for lover, 41–42
Adolescent, 185–190
Affairs, 6, 26–27, 51, 172–173
Africa, AIDS in, 165
AIDS (see Acquired immunodeficiency syndrome)
AIDS-related complex (ARC), xvii, 149
Alcohol:
  adolescent and, 188
  danger of, 135
Amyl nitrite, 135–136
Anal intercourse:
  AIDS and, 154
  condoms and, 71, 154
  lubrication and, 71, 154
  nonoxynol-9 and, 78
Anal stimulation, 91
Anonymous testing, 157
Antibodies, HIV, xvii, 156
ARC (see AIDS-related complex)
Art of seduction, 121–122
Artificial insemination, 168
Assertiveness, 7
  asking for what you want, 32
  detachment and, 38
  phrase guide for, 23–24
  social ethic and, 25–27
  unsafe situation and, 35
Awareness of self, 12

Bank, sperm, 168
Barrier contraceptive, 78
Bill of rights, 139
Birth control, 78, 170–171
Bisexual man, 10, 21, 39, 173–174
Bite:
  human, 181–182
  mosquito, 155
Blame of self, 10–11
Bleach, 81, 163

Blood:
  donation of, 155
  menstrual, 84–85, 163, 164
  spread of AIDS and, 152–153
Blood brother, 181
Body decoration, 125–126
Body fluids, 132
  condom disposal and, 74–75
  definition of, xvii
  kissing and, 187
  partner at risk and, 171
  petting and, 184–185
  play and, 123
Boundaries, setting of, 34–35, 41
Breath-holding, 111
Butyl nitrite, 135–136

Caffeine, 136
*Candida albicans,* 160
Carrier of virus, 6
Celibacy, xvii, 4, 6
Chemical substances, 135–136, 188
Child:
  AIDS education and, 176–192
    adolescent and, 185–190
    age 4–8 years, 180–182
    preschool age, 179–180
    preteen and, 182–185
  spread of AIDS to, 153
Chlamydial infection, 160
Chocolate, 136
Classmate with AIDS, 181
Clitoris, 107
  dental dam and, 80
  extragenital sex and, 44
  G spot and, 90
  self-stimulation and, 104
  talking with children about, 179
Co-dependency, 28–29, 113–114
Cocaine, 135
College-age adult, 190–192
Commitment, safe-sex (*see* Safe-sex commitment, personal)
Communication, 23–24, 29–38, 112
  about AIDS, 175
  about sex, 9
  condoms and, 88
  latex protection and, 82–85
  outercourse and, 55–56
  to develop intimacy, 29–35
  touching and, 47
  with children and adolescents, 176–190
  with self, 8–17
Condom:
  adolescent's questions about, 187–188
  buying of, 67–68
Condom (*Cont.*):
  disposal of, 74–75
  eroticizing of, 85–88
  manufacturers and distributors of, 207–208
  safer use of, 67–75
  shopping for, 65–67
  talking with children about, 177, 183–184
Confidential testing, 27, 36, 157
Conscious self-focus, 12
Contamination and spread of AIDS, 152–153
Contraceptives:
  AIDS protection and, 170–171
  barrier, 78
Counseling, 194–196
Crack, 135
Cream, contraceptive:
    diaphragm and, 79
    nonoxynol-9 and, 77–78
Cunnilingus, xvi, 79
  (*See also* Oral-genital sex)

Dam, dental, 79–81
    eroticizing of, 88–89
Danger, physical, 24–25
Decoration, body, 125–126
Deep kissing, 187
Denial of AIDS, 37–38
Dental dam, 79–81
  eroticizing of, 88–89
Diaphragm, 78–79
Diarrhea, 165
Discrimination, 157
Do-it-yourself AIDS antibody test kit, 158
Donation of blood, 155
Drugs:
  AIDS treatment and, 162
  intravenous:
    AIDS risk and, 162
    AIDS testing and, 158
    contaminated needles and, 152
    definition of, xvii
    education of child and, 183–186
    lesbian relationship and, 163
    partner's use of, 20–21, 39, 172
    re-entering dating scene and, 169
  stimulant and depressant, 135–136

Eating, 131–132
Education:
  AIDS, 202–205
    adolescents and, 185–190
    college-age adult and, 190–192
    preschool age child and, 179–180

Education: AIDS (*Cont.*):
preteens and, 182–185
young child and, 180–182
mass, 173
slogans and, 64
Electric vibrator, 105–106
ELISA Test, xvii, 156–157
Emotions, 28, 91–92, 116, 137
body memory and, 46
condom use and, 64
disconnection from, 9
play and, 137
self-pleasure and, 113
trust and, 169
Epidemic, 175
Erect penis, putting condom on, 72
Erotica:
enjoyment of, 132–134
mail-order houses for, 208
Eroticism of latex:
condoms and, 85–88
dental dams and, 88–89
gloves and, 89–91
Esteem, self-, 15–16
Etiquette of sex, 5–8
Evaluation, safe-sex, xv–xvi
Extragenital stimulation, 43–63
adolescents and, 186
creative outercourse and, 50–56
extragenital matrix and, 60, 62–63
extragenital sensitivity and, 58–60
partner and, 50
personal safe-sex commitment and, 61
sexual norms and, 56–58
talking with children about, 185
touching, 45–49

False intimacy, 27–28
False test results, 156
Family therapy, 197–198
Fantasy:
masturbation and, 107–109
safe-sex, 118
Fear of AIDS:
abusive relationship and, 28–29
instant monogamy and, 27–28
Fellatio, xvi
(*See also* Oral-genital sex)
Fingers, self-stimulation and, 103–105
Flaccid penis, putting condom on, 72
Fluids, body (*see* Body fluids)
Foam, contraceptive, 78
Food, 129–132
Forced sex, 12
Forgiveness of self, 10
French kissing, 187
Frustration, teasing and, 122–123
Future fantasy, 108

G spot, 44, 89–91
Genital warts, 160
Gland, prostate, 90
Gloves, latex, 80, 81, 185
G spot and, 89
Gonorrhea:
decreased incidence of, 173
symptoms of, 160
Grafenberg spot, 89–91
Group, peer, 198–199
Group therapy, 198
Guilt, 35, 96

Herpes:
cure and, 151
symptoms of, 160
High-risk behaviors, xvii
AIDS and, 154
definition of, xvi–xvii
sexually transmitted diseases and, 152–153, 158, 169–170
High-risk groups, 159, 162
History:
partner's, 21–25
self-pleasure, 116–117
HIV (*see* Human immunodeficiency virus)
Homosexual woman partner:
AIDS and, 163
latex products and, 84–85
safety of, 19–20
Hotline, AIDS, 202
Human immunodeficiency virus, xvii, 148–152
antibody testing and, 156
carrier of, 6
casual contact and, 154
kissing and, 49
(*See also* Acquired immune deficiency syndrome)
Husband, bisexual, 173–174
Hydrogen peroxide, 81

Individual therapy, 197
Infant, 153
Infection:
human immunodeficiency virus and, 148–151
antibody testing and, 156, 194–195
casual contact and, 154, 162
opportunistic, xvii, 148–150
Infibulation, 91, 165
Ingestion of nonoxynol-9, 78

Insemination, artificial, 168
Insurance, 36–37, 157
Intercourse, 67–74, 147, 184, 187
  anal:
    AIDS and, 154
    lubrication and, 71
    nonoxynol-9 and, 78
  condoms and (*see* Condoms)
  danger of, 24
  initiation of, 55
  limits of, 8
  masturbation and, 100, 102
  other options for, 43–63
  out-of-bed, 123–125
  responsibility and, 138
    (*See also* Extragenital stimulation)
Intimacy, false, 27–28
Intravenous drugs (*see* Drugs, intravenous)

Jelly, contraceptive:
  diaphragm and, 79
  nonoxynol-9 and, 78

Kegel exercise, 111
Kissing, 187
  AIDS virus and, 49, 154, 187
Kit, AIDS antibody test, 158

Latex, 64–95
  communication about, 82–85
  condoms:
    failure of, 76–77
    safe use of, 67–75
    sexually transmitted disease and, 75–76
    shopping for, 65–67
  dental dams and, 79–81
  diaphragms and, 78–79
  eroticizing of, 85–92
  foams, jellies, creams and, 78
  gloves and, 80, 81, 185
  household items and, 81
  lingerie and, 88–89
  nonoxynol-9 and, 77–78
Lesbian relationship:
  AIDS and, 163
  latex products and, 84–85
  safety of, 19–20
Lingerie, latex, 88–89
Long-term relationship, 172–175
Love, 137
  body memory and, 46–47
  of self, 17
  sex and, 9
  teenager and, 187

Lubricant:
  anal stimulation and, 91
  condom and, 69, 71, 86
  latex-gloves and, 81, 89–90
  nonoxynol-9 and, 77–78

Mail-order houses, 208
Marijuana, 135
  adolescent and, 188
Massage, 46–47
Masturbation, 96–116
  fantasy and, 107–109, 118
  fingers and, 103–105
  learning how, 109–112
  myth versus information about, 98–101
  partner and, 112–116
  self-pleasure history and, 116–117
  taboos concerning, 97–98
  thigh pressure and, 106
  vibrators and, 105–106
  water play and, 106–107
Maternal-child transmission of AIDS, 153, 166–168
Menstrual blood, 84–85, 163, 164
Monogamy, 19, 136–137
  definition of, xvii
  infected partner and, 4
  instant, 26–28
  trustworthy, 6
Mood-altering substances, 135–136
Mosquito bite, 155
Myths about masturbation, 98–101

N-9 (*see* Nonoxynol-9)
Needle, contaminated (*see* Drugs, intravenous)
Negative relationship, 28–29
New partner, 8
  romance and, 51–52
  safer sex with, 171
Night sweats, 165
Nonoxynol-9, 71, 77–79, 81

Oil-based lubricant, 69
Ongoing relationship, 25–29, 172–175
Opportunistic infections, xviii, 149
Oral dam, 79–81
Oral-genital sex:
  AIDS and, 153–154
  dental dam and, 79
Orgasm, 103–106, 108, 111–113, 127–128
  drugs and, 135
  G spot and, 89
  as goal, 138

Orgasm (*Cont.*):
  masturbation and (*see* Masturbation)
  play and, 122–123
  pleasure mantra and, 16
Outdoor sex, 124–125
Outercourse, 43–63
  (*See also* Extragenital stimulation)

Partner:
  communicating with, 20–25, 29–35
  HIV positive, 166–167
  new, 8, 171
  play and, 120–144
  solo sex and, 112–116
  surrogate, 53
Peer group, 198–199
Penis:
  condom and, 67, 74, 85–87
  focus away from, 54
  talking with children about, 179, 183
Permission of partner, 50
Personal safe-sex commitment:
  awareness and self-worth, 18
  extragenital sex and, 61
  latex products and, 95
  play and, 142
  right relationship and, 42
  self-pleasuring and, 118–119
Petting, 184–185
Phone sex, 52–53
Phrase guide (*see* Pocket phrase guide)
Physical danger, 24–25
Placenta, 153
Plastic wrap, 79–80
Play:
  chemical substances and, 135–136
  dressing and undressing, 125–126
  erotica and, 132–134
  food and, 129–132
  initiating of, 121–123
  out-of-bed encounters and, 123–125
  responsibility and, 140–142
  safe sex and, 136–139
  sense of smell and, 127–129
  teaching partner to, 120–144
Pleasure:
  play and, 137–138
  responsibility and, 140–142
Pocket phrase guide:
  condom use and, 83–84
  initiating outercourse, 55–56
  initiating relationships, 23–24
  self-pleasuring with partner and, 115
Poppers, 135–136
Post-test counseling, 166, 194–195
Pregnancy, AIDS and, 166–169
Preschool child, 179–180
Preteen child, 182–185
Pre-test counseling, 166, 194
Prevention, 137
Progress chart, relationship, 40–41
Prostate gland stimulation, 90
Psychotherapy, 196–198

Questions:
  for potential partner, 20
  for safe partner, 39–40

Rape:
  AIDS risk and, 164–165
  memory of, 46
Receptacle tip of condom, 70
Rectum:
  AIDS and, 154
  fragility of, 91
Relationship:
  long-term, 25–29, 172–175
  new, 20–25
    (*See also* New partner)
  right, 19–42
    communication and, 29–36
    denial of AIDS and, 37–38
    guidelines for, 25–29
    progress chart and, 40–41
    protection of partner and, 36–37
    question to ask potential partner, 20–25
    questions concerning, 39–40
Relationship therapy, 197
Responsibility:
  play and, 138–139
  pleasure and, 140–142
Rights:
  bill of, 139
  to safe sex, 23
Risk:
  adolescents and, 185–190
  children and, 176–185
  definition of, xv–xvii, 152–155
  geography and, 161
  heterosexuality and, 161
  intravenous drug use and, 161
  pregnancy and, 166–169
  women and, 161–165
Road map (*see* Safe-sex road map; Safer-sex road map)
Roll, oral condom, 87–88
Romance, 51–52

Safe sex:
  attitudes and, 3–18
    awareness and self-worth, 17

Safe sex (Cont.)
behaviors, xvi, 171
journal keeping and, 17–18
new etiquette and, 5–8
self-esteem and, 15–17
self-forgiveness and, 10–11
self-knowledge and, 8–10
self-mirroring and, 14–15
bill of rights for, 139
definition of, xvi, xviii, 153
pregnancy and, 167
right relationship and, 19–42
right to, 23
self-awareness and, 12–13
single person and, 169–172
Safe-sex commitment, personal:
awareness and self-worth, 18
extragenital sex and, 61
latex products and, 95
play and, 142
right relationship and, 42
self-pleasuring and, 118–119
Safe-sex evaluation, xv–xvi
Safe-sex road map:
awareness and self-worth, 17–18
extragenital sensitivity, 63
pleasure and responsibility, 140–141
safe relationships, 38–42
self-pleasure and, 116–119
Safer sex:
behavior and, xvi–xviii, 67–75, 169–170, 174
condom use and, 67–75, 85–88
definition of, xviii, 153
dental dam and, 79–81, 89
diaphragm and, 78
latex gloves and, 81, 90
nonoxynal-9 and, 77–88
Safer-sex road map:
latex and, 92–95
pleasure and responsibility and, 140–142
Safety seal on condom, 74
Saliva, xvii, 49, 79, 181, 187
Scent, 128
Seduction, art of safe, 121–122
Self-awareness, 12
Self-blame, 10–11
Self-esteem, 15–16
Self-forgiveness, 10
Self-image, directed, 14–15
Self-knowledge, 8–17
Self-mirroring, 14–15
Self-pleasuring (*see* Masturbation)
Sensation, creation of, 48–49
Sensitivity, extragenital, 58–60
Setting boundaries, 34–35
Sex:
as energy, 8–9
etiquette of safe, 5–8
extragenital (*see* Extragenital stimulation)
forced, 12
AIDS risk and, 164–165
memory of, 46
oral-genital:
AIDS and, 153–154
dental dam and, 79
outdoor, 124–125
phone, 52–53
solo (*see* Masturbation)
with therapist, 200
Sex education, 176–192
(*See also* Education)
Sex therapy, 195–196
Sexual imagery, 132–134
Sexual norm, 56–58
Sexually transmitted disease:
adolescent and, 191
condoms and, 75–76
definition of, xviii, 159
signs and symptoms of, 159–160
Shopping for condoms, 65–67
Slogans versus education, 64
Smell, 127–129
Solo sex (*see* Masturbation)
Sperm bank, 168
Spermicidal jelly, 77–78, 171
Spermicide, 69, 81, 93–96
definition of, xviii
nonoxynol-9, 71, 77–79, 81
talking with children about, 183, 188
Spot, G, 89–91
Stimulation:
anal, 91
extragenital (*see* Extragenital stimulation)
of G spot, 89
of self (*see* Masturbation)
Storing of condom, 67–68
Support group, AIDS, 202–205
Surrogate partner, 53
Syphilis, 160

Taboos concerning masturbation, 97–98
Teasing, 122
Telephone sex, 52–53
Testing:
AIDS, 36–37, 155–158
anonymity of, 157
confidentiality of, 157
ELISA Test, xvii, 156

Testing: AIDS (*Cont.*):
false results, 156
importance of counseling with, 166, 194
of partners, 27
Western Blot Test, xviii, 156
of condoms, 68–69
Therapist, trust in, 199–201
Therapy:
psychotherapy and, 196–198
resources for, 210
safe, 199–201
sex, 195–196
Thigh pressure, 105–106
Tongue kissing, 187
Touching:
of partner, 45–49
(*See also* Extragenital stimulation; G spot; Massage)
of self, 96–116
(*See also* Masturbation)
Transfusion, 10, 21, 39
safety of, 155
spread of AIDS and, 152–153
Trichomonas, 160

Uterus, 78–79

Vaccine for AIDS, 151
Vagina, 43, 45
condom and, 67, 74
dental dam and, 80
lubrication and, 69, 71
self-stimulation of, 104
spermicide and, 77–79
talking with children about, 179, 183
Vaginitis, 160
Vasectomy, 174
Vibrators, 105–106
distributors of, 208
Visualization:
asking for what you want and, 32–33
self-forgiveness and, 11
Vulva, 80, 104, 110

Warts, genital, 160
Water play:
bubblebath and, 53–54
masturbation and, 106–107
Water-soluble lubricant, 69
Western Blot test, xviii, 156
Women and AIDS, 161–165
resources for, 205–207
Wrap, plastic, 79–80